HANDS-ON

DISCOVERY CENTER ACTIVITIES

FOR PRESCHOOL CHILDREN

LORRAINE CLANCY

THE CENTER FOR APPLIED
RESEARCH IN EDUCATION
West Nyack, New York 10995

© 1993 by
THE CENTER FOR APPLIED
RESEARCH IN EDUCATION
West Nyack, NY

10 9 8 7 6 5 4

Library of Congress Cataloging-in-Publication Data

Clancy, Lorraine.
  Hands-on discovery center activities for preschool children /
Lorraine Clancy.
    p.   cm.

C8107-9
ISBN 0-87628-810-7

  1. Education, Preschool—United States—Activity programs.
2. Classroom learning centers—United States. 3. Learning by
discovery.   I. Title.
LB1139.35.A37C53   1993
372.21—dc20   93-10642
                                                              CIP

**THE CENTER FOR APPLIED RESEARCH
IN EDUCATION**
West Nyack, NY 10994

On the World Wide Web at http://www.phdirect.com

Printed in the United States of America

**Dedicated to a happy childhood
for all children**

ABOUT THE AUTHOR

LORRAINE CLANCY received her B.S. degree in Early Childhood Education from the State University at Old Westbury, New York. She is presently teaching preschool at St. Joseph's School in Garden City, New York, a program she began in 1980.

Mrs. Clancy has taught arts and crafts workshops for elementary teachers, as well as summer classes for children. She is a charter member of the Early Childhood Circle of the Diocese of Rockville Centre.

Mrs. Clancy is also the author of *Seasonal Arts and Crafts Activities for Early Childhood* (Parker Publishing Company, 1988) and *Preschool Teacher's Month-by-Month Activities Program* (The Center for Applied Research in Education, 1991).

About This Book

Hands-On Discovery Center Activities for Preschool Children gives you the essential ingredients to make your preschool classroom and program more exciting and effective. It is packed with hundreds of hands-on materials, projects, and reproducibles that will make children eager to explore the centers each preschool day.

You'll find these Discovery Centers an ideal way to arrange your room and your program to meet the needs and ambitions of your preschoolers. Children, especially three- to five-year-olds, need an orderly physical environment in which to experience the joys of discovery and learning. Organizing your room into centers gives you a practical way to encourage independent learning by each child as well as provide for individual differences in interests, backgrounds, and abilities.

All of the Discovery Centers in this resource are designed to use standard classroom supplies or easily obtainable materials that relate to preschoolers' natural curiosity about their environment. The activities invite children to become involved and develop their social, cognitive, and motor skills as they experience the world around them.

The five Discovery Centers in this book are designed to encourage discovery and learning:

- The **Nature and Science Discovery Center** encourages your preschoolers to observe, learn, and share their curiosity about the world around them.
- The **Creative Arts Discovery Center**—through varied media—appeals to the innate artistic nature of children.
- The **Numbers Discovery Center** is a place where children start building a foundation for the world of numbers in their future.
- The **Shapes and Letters Discovery Center** provides pre-reading activities that are enjoyable learning experiences.
- The **Five Senses Discovery Center** provides children with numerous opportunities to experience the environment with their eyes, nose, mouth, ears, and fingers.

Using this resource, you can easily and inexpensively equip and organize your Discovery Centers to suit your own particular classroom and curriculum needs. Based on your class size and the age of your children, you can choose to divide the children into small groups and direct them to use the various centers or allow them to select the center of their choice. A Discovery Center "Management Sheet" is included for each center to make record keeping easy.

Each Discovery Center includes a variety of suggested activities and projects. You may wish to set up one or two activities in each center and have the children visit them in groups each day. The children will enjoy the independence of "playing" at each Discovery Center while you help them to experience many hands-on activities and to explore the meanings behind them.

Organizing into Discovery Centers gives you the opportunity to help children with their skills development in an enjoyable and efficient manner. Discover these centers and you'll love preschool as much as your children!

Lorraine Clancy

Why Have Discovery Centers in Your Preschool Classroom?

Preschool children abound in curiosity and energy. They want to get their hands on and into everything they see that looks interesting to them. They are fascinated by things that move, change, and grow. Preschool teachers can demonstrate and talk about all the wonders of their world, but preschoolers want to *experience* these phenomena for themselves.

Since children absorb 20% of what they hear, 30% of what they see, and 70% of what they do, their most successful learning will be in the *doing*. As the children progress through these Discovery Centers, they will be developing a myriad of early childhood skills.

As the school year progresses, the children's awareness of the world around them will grow along with their fine-motor, eye-hand coordination skills, and vocabulary. Awareness of colors and shapes of things in their environment increases on a daily basis. They are willing to explore, to try the unknown, and to use their senses to the fullest. The joy of learning is evidenced in their obvious positive self-esteem and enthusiasm.

The foundation for successful future schooling begins with hands-on experiences in preschool. By allowing children the time and opportunity to explore these preschool Discovery Centers, you are providing them with creative learning experiences that will become the foundation for concept development.

How to Manage
the Discovery Centers

The Discovery Centers' activities are meant to be used in whatever way best suits you, your children, and your program. You might want to set up two or three centers at one time and change them each month. Or perhaps you want all five centers going on at the same time. You might pick and choose among each center's activities that support or enhance a particular concept you wish to explore with the children, or you may set up a chosen center at a special time of the year and have the children participate in all of the suggested activities. As you become familiar with the Discovery Centers and their activities, you will be able to decide how to set up the centers and how many activities to have in each center.

Suggested Floor Plan

If you choose to set up all five Discovery Centers as shown in the suggested floor plan, you may divide your children into groups of two or three. The set up of all five centers gives the children maximum exposure to the wide variety of activities contained in this book.

Management Sheets

Keep track of the children's use of the centers on the Management Sheet that accompanies each Discovery Center. Make copies of the sheet and, on the diagonal lines at the top, write the projects or activities you intend to set up. Then write in the children's names in the left-hand column. Put a check mark in the box below each activity when you have assigned that particular activity to the child. Using these Management Sheets will give you a clear picture of the experiences that each child has explored and what new Discovery Center to assign. The sheets will also be of great help when you have parent conferences.

Mix the groups of children so that all the children will have the opportunity to explore the center with different classmates.

Suggested Preschool Day Schedule

A typical preschool day is 2½ hours. Here is a suggested schedule that you may use or blend into your present organization of the day.

9:00-9:15	Arrival, Greetings, Chatting, Puzzles
9:15-9:30	Opening Exercises, Attendance, Calendar, Classroom Jobs, Discovery Center Assignments
9:30-10:00	Discovery Center Activities
10:00-10:10	Straighten-up Centers
10:10-10:20	Story Time
10:20-10:30	Snack Time, Show and Tell
10:30-11:00	Housekeeping Corner, Block Corner, Classroom Toys
11:00-11:25	(*will vary each day*) Whole Group Songs, Poems, Fingerplays, Outdoor Play, Gym, Movement Exercises, Rhythm Band
11:25-11:30	Getting ready to go home

During the time allotted for "Discovery Center Assignments," you should present any new center activities or review those that have been experienced by some but not all of the children. This review not only reinforces the project's objectives, but allows for input from the children who have completed the particular center's activity. Many lively discussions will arise at this time! Allow the children time to express their particular reactions or thoughts about each new or reviewed Discovery Center project. Then let the children explore their centers.

A Final Word

By providing an intriguing environment and provocative materials—as well as space and time—the children will see the great fun it is to discover (and learn) new connections and creations—whether working side by side or on their own!

Suggested Floor Plan For Five Discovery Centers

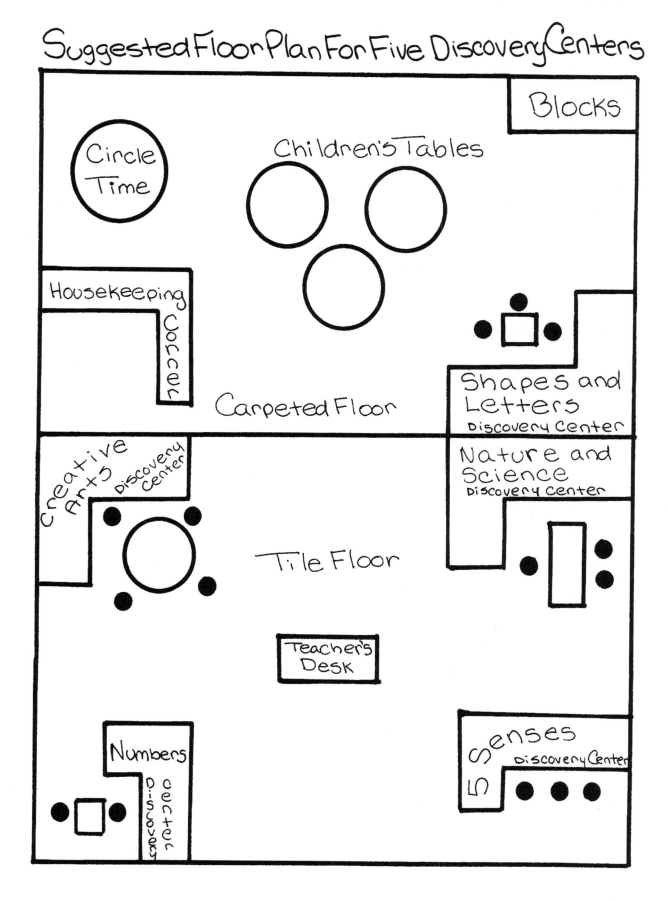

Acknowledgments

It is with utmost sincerity that I would like to acknowledge my 13 years' worth of wonderful Saint Joseph's children, who continue to light up my life.

Contents

I. Nature and Science Discovery Center

With their natural sense of wonder and insatiable curiosity, young children make enthusiastic scientists. Handling common substances, such as rocks, sand, and water, gives them the opportunity to react and interact with things that are a part of their everyday lives. The hands-on activities presented in this section introduce children to the amazing and exciting world of nature and science while they encourage further explorations!

Nature and Science Discovery Center Management Sheet

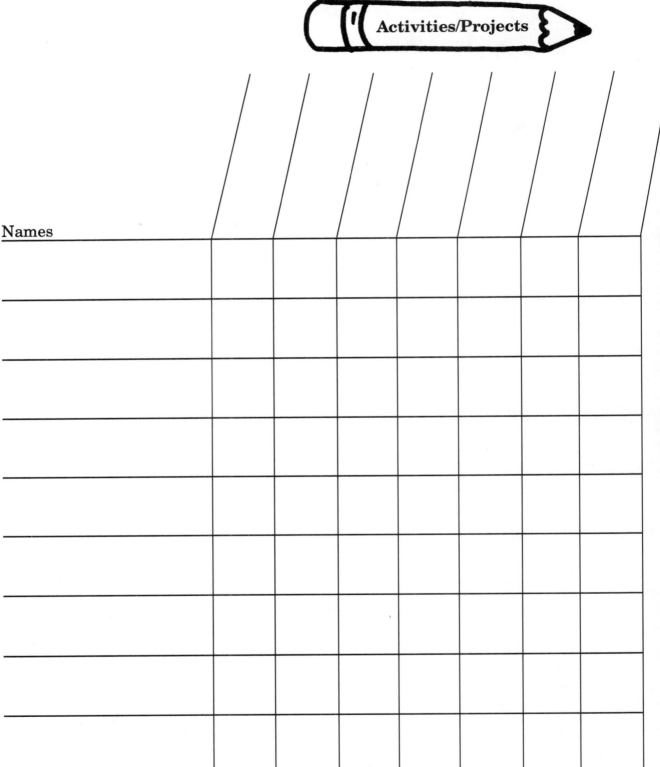

Activities/Projects

Names

Nature and Science Discovery Center Management Sheet

Activities/Projects

Names

I-A. MAGNETISM

Purpose

The children will play with a variety of magnets and discover their properties through hands-on experiences enabling them to see and feel magnetism. They will feel like poles repelling each other and unlike poles attracting each other. Through their own experiments, the children will also discover which things magnets "stick to" and "do not stick to."

Getting Started

1. Provide the children with a variety of magnets, including magnetic shower curtain liners, decorative refrigerator magnets, magnetic closures on pocketbooks, and magnetic advertising signs that stick to cars, vans, and trucks.

2. Let the children explore around the classroom to see how magnets will stick to some things and not to others. Can a magnet pick up a paper clip? What happens when more paper clips are used? Have some iron filings available and encourage the children to experiment making pictures with the filings and a magnet.

3. Divide the children into smaller groups (the number of groups depends upon the number of magnets you have) and have each group member take turns finding one thing in the classroom to which his or her magnet is attracted. When each child in the group has found one, provide the children with paper and crayons to draw the item while the next group goes. When everyone is finished drawing their items, then, one by one, the group members can share their pictures and name their objects for the rest of the class. (Of course, it does not matter if the next group finds the same objects, but encourage exploration to find different items.)

Activity IA-1. The "Attract/Does Not Attract" Box

Materials Needed

- shoe box set up as shown
- small box with a variety of items that magnets attract and do not attract
- magnet

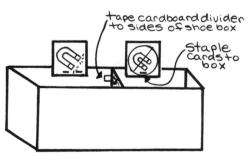

Directions for Children

1. Take an item out of the box and "test" it with the magnet to see if the magnet will attract ("stick to") it or not.
2. After testing the item, put it in the appropriate side of the shoe box.
3. Continue testing the rest of the items.

Going Further

1. Gather a variety of different shapes of magnets. Explain that magnets often get their names from their shape, for example, horseshoe, ring, bar, block, and disc. Have the children trace around each magnet on separate 3″ × 5″ cards, and color in each magnet. The children can then say the name of each magnet with you as you all hold up the same cards.

2. Make a "Magnet Collage." Divide the class into small groups and give each group member a piece of white construction paper and a variety of magnets to share. Have them trace the shapes all over their paper and then color the magnet shapes. When they are finished, the children can name the magnet shapes for their classmates.

Activity I-A2. Jumping Magnets

Materials Needed

- collection of disc magnets (you can get these from old magnetic shower curtain liners)

Directions for Children

1. Set out the magnets on a table.
2. Pick up one magnet and hold it over another magnet. Do not touch it to the magnet on the table.
3. Does the magnet on the table jump up to meet the one in your hand or does it move away?
4. Do the same experiment with the other magnets on the table.

Going Further

Gather and display a variety of common rocks. Add to the collection a piece of Magnetite (a natural magnet, also called lodestone). Magnetite can be bought in the science department of an education store or at a rock and mineral store.

Have the children experiment with the magnetic quality of the magnetite as opposed to the other rocks. Explain that in ancient times, magnetite was considered to be a "magic stone." It was discovered in a country in Asia Minor called Magnesia. The word "magnet" comes from "Magnesia."

Activity I-A3. Buried Treasure

Materials Needed

- copy of "Pirate Hat" worksheet
- 2″ × 12″ construction paper
- strong magnet
- assortment of small iron and non-iron "treasure" (buttons, paper clips, nuts and bolts, small plastic comb, bobby pins, plastic spoon, wooden beads, etc.) buried in a shallow box filled with one-half inch of sand
- stapler

Directions for Children

1. Color the pirate hat and cut it out.
2. Staple it (your teacher will help) to the construction paper band to fit around your head.
3. Wear your pirate hat and search for the "magnetic treasure" by passing the magnet over the sand.
4. After you have found all of the magnetic treasure, you can dig up the non-magnetic objects.

Going Further

1. Look at the pile of items that the magnet picked up. What do you notice about these items? Pick them up again with your magnet. What are they made of?

Now look at the pile of items that the magnet would not pick up. Try to pick them up again with your magnet. What is each of these items made of?

2. You might have the children investigate the meaning of the skull and crossbones on the pirate hat. Talk about how the symbol is now used as a warning sign, as on poison.

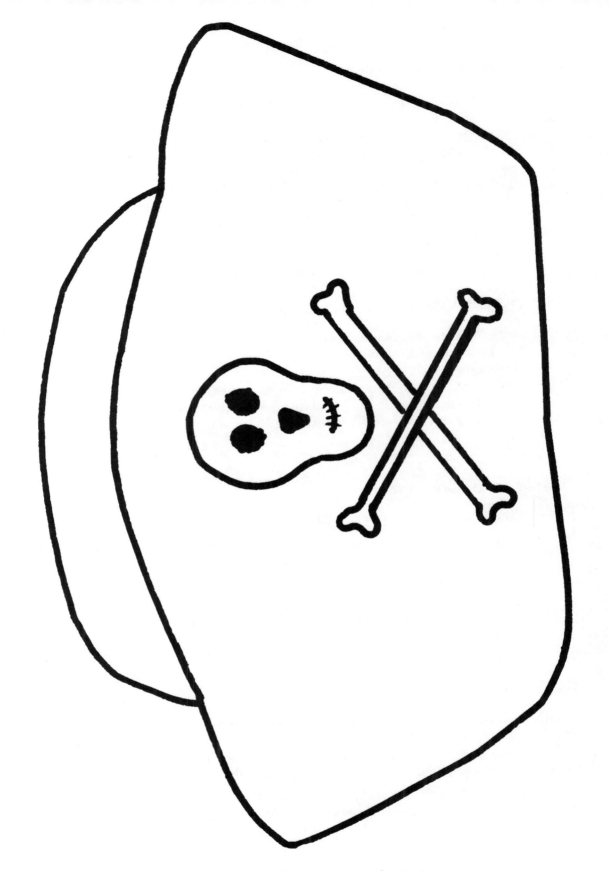

Activity I-A4. Magnetic Pyramid

Materials Needed

- magnetic marbles
- shoe box

Directions for Children

1. Make a line of four marbles in the shoe box.
2. Line up three marbles on top of the four marbles.
3. Next, line up two marbles.
4. Then, add one marble on top.

Going Further

How many more pyramids can you make? Can you make different structures with your marbles?

Activity I-A5. Floating Rings

Materials Needed

- magnetic rings
- six-inch wooden dowel

Directions for Children

1. Put one magnetic ring on the dowel.
2. Put another ring on the dowel. If this second ring attracts to the first, take it off, turn it over, and put it back on the dowel.
3. Observe how it "floats" above the first magnet.
4. Continue as above with the other ring magnets.

Going Further

Explain that magnets "pull together" or "away" from each other. Demonstrate this by pretending that your hands are both magnets. Your palms can be the "pull together" side and the back of your hands can be the "push away" side.

Have the children pretend to be a magnet with their hands while they say "pull together" and "push away." Allow them to experiment with real magnets.

Activity I-A6. 3-D Designs

Materials Needed

- variety of metal stampings, metal washers, paper clips, and metal nuts and bolts
- two large rectangular magnets

Directions for Children

1. Set the two bar magnets about five inches apart.
2. Use the metal materials to build a three-dimensional design between the two magnets.

Going Further

Show a magnetic field on an overhead projector. Carefully sprinkle iron filings onto the glass surface of an overhead projector. (Don't allow any filings to get under the glass because scratches on the glass can result.) Cover them with a rigid piece of plastic. Let the children use various shaped magnets to make the filings move into "lines of force." Project these dramatic images on a screen or wall.

Activity I-A7. Magnetic Maze

Materials Needed

- copy of "Magnetic Maze" worksheet glued onto oaktag
- disc magnet
- bar magnet

Directions for Children

1. Put the disc magnet by the arrow at the top of the maze.
2. Hold the worksheet in one hand.
3. With your other hand, hold the bar magnet and put it under the disc magnet to move it through the maze.

Going Further

Show the children a piece of magnetite and explain that it is called a "natural" magnet because it is made of iron ore from the ground. (See Activity I-A2.) Then show a magnet with which the children have been experimenting and explain that most of our magnets are made in a factory (from ceramic or metal alloy) and are called "man-made" or "people-made" magnets. Demonstrate that both natural and people-made magnets have "pull-together" and "push-away" qualities.

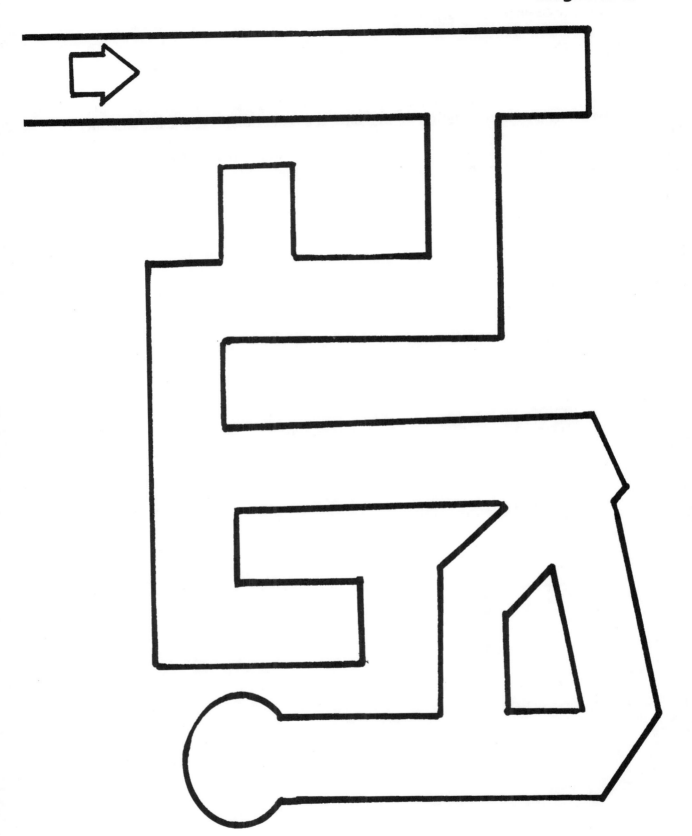

Activity I-A8. Can a Magnet's Pull Go Through Air, Water, Sand, and Paper?

Materials Needed

- four paper clips
- four paper cups cut down to 1½"
- water
- sand
- piece of paper
- bar magnet

Directions for Children

1. Line up the four cups.
2. Put a paper clip in each cup.
3. The first cup will be for pulling through air.
4. Add ¾ of an inch of water to the second cup.
5. Add ¼ of an inch of sand to the third cup.
6. Lay a small piece of paper on top of the last cup.
7. Now, experiment attracting the paper clips with the bar magnet. Hold the magnet above the first cup. Can it pull the paper clip through the air?
8. Hold the magnet just above the water in the second cup. Can the magnet pull the paper clip through the water?
9. Move to the third cup. Hold the magnet at the surface of the sand. Can the magnet pull the paper clip through the sand?
10. Touch the magnet to the paper on the last cup. Can it pull the paper clip through the paper?

Going Further

Gather materials of different thicknesses, such as corrugated cardboard, oaktag, construction paper, foil, plastic wrap, small pieces of wood, and so on. Lay each one on the top of a different paper clip. With a bar or horseshoe magnet, try to attract the paper clip through each material. Encourage the children to discuss the results so that they can have the experience of talking about scientific explorations.

Activity I-A9. Paper Clip Art

Materials Needed

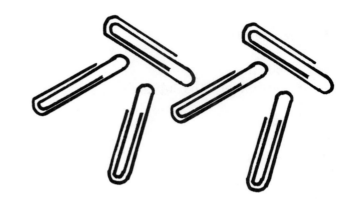

- margarine lid
- paper clip
- glue
- sheet of white paper
- tempera paint
- safety scissors

Directions for Children

1. Cut the piece of paper to fit inside the margarine lid.
2. Glue it in place.
3. Put one-half teaspoon of tempera paint into the center of the paper.
4. Drop the paper clip into the center of the paint.
5. Hold the magnet under the lid.
6. Move the paper clip around the lid to make a "magnetic" design.

Going Further

Instead of one color paint, have the children use ¼ teaspoon of red tempera paint and ¼ teaspoon of yellow tempera paint. The moving paper clip will mix these two primary colors so that the children will see orange (a secondary color) emerge. Let the children experiment with other primary colors and encourage them to predict what will happen when the different colors are mixed.

Activity I-A10. Help Barney Find His Home

Materials Needed

- copy of "Barney" worksheet glued onto oaktag
- two bar magnets
- 3″ × 5″ card
- crayons
- tape

Directions for Children

1. Color the worksheet.
2. Draw a picture of a dog on the card.
3. Tape your picture of a dog named Barney onto one of the bar magnets as shown on the worksheet.
4. Put Barney at the bottom of your worksheet and hold the worksheet with one hand.
5. Hold the other magnet underneath the worksheet where Barney is standing. Now move Barney around the streets.
6. See how the magnet can "pull" right through the worksheet!

Going Further

1. *Magnetic Fields*: Explain that the "push away" and "pull together" powers of a magnet are called the magnet's "magnetic field" and cannot be seen. Demonstrate the concept of this "invisible" power with two disc magnets. Lay one on the table and hold the other directly above this one. If the magnets' sides facing each other are *unlike* (North/South) poles, the magnet on the table will "jump" up and attach itself to the other magnet. If the poles are *like* (North/North, South/South) poles, the magnet on the table will stay where it is or move away. Let the children "chase" the magnet on the table with the one you are holding.

2. *"Seeing" Magnetic Fields*: Place a piece of paper, thin rigid plastic, or oaktag on top of a bar magnet. Sprinkle iron filings on top of the paper and shake the paper slightly. The filings will arrange themselves in a pattern showing the magnetic fields. Let the children take turns dropping the iron filings on the paper and shaking it. Let the children also have a chance to manipulate the magnets in order to see that a magnet's pulling power is stronger at its poles than in its middle area.

I-B. SEEDS

Purpose

The children will explore the fascinating world of seeds and begin to discover the vast variety of seeds that exist in our world and their tremendous potential. Breaking apart a flower seed pocket, collecting the seeds of trees, as well as cutting vegetables to find their seeds, will expand children's knowledge and add to their comprehension of where seeds come from. Planting seeds, taking care of seedlings, and observing their growth will foster an awareness of the miracle of nature's reproduction process.

Getting Started

1. Bring in packages of vegetable and flower seeds. The picture of the flower or vegetable will be on the front panel. Have the children shake the packages so they can hear the sound each package of seeds makes. Explain that if you plant the seeds, you will grow the vegetable or flower pictured on the front of the package.

   Open each package and let the children look at the seeds. Spread out the seeds on some small styrofoam meat trays, and glue the package's picture next to the seeds. Explain that each flower and vegetable makes its own seeds. Display these at the "Nature and Science Discovery Center."

2. Bring in a vegetable (green pepper), a flower (marigold), and a fruit (apple). Cut open the pepper and show the children all the seeds inside the pepper. Do the same for the apple and the marigold.

3. Announce to the parents that you will be studying seeds with their preschoolers. Ask the parents to send in a vegetable or fruit that has seeds in it, and to save any seeds they find while they are cooking, gardening or simply come across during the course of their day. Make a large chart on posterboard with pictures of the fruits, vegetables, and flowers that correspond to the seeds the children bring in. Attach a plastic sandwich bag below each picture. Have the children put the seeds they bring in from home in the appropriate bag.

Activity I-B1. Flower Seed Pockets

Materials Needed

- seed pockets from marigolds, daisies, and impatiens (collect the seed pockets from garden flowers in the late fall)

- copy of "Flower Seed Pockets" worksheet
- magnifying glass
- crayons or markers
- glue

Directions for Children

1. Look closely at the pictures of the flowers and the location and shape of each flower's seed pocket.
2. Look at a seed pocket and decide which pictured flower it belongs to.
3. Break apart the seed pocket.
4. Examine the seeds with a magnifying glass. Note their color, shape, and size.
5. Color the picture of the flower with crayons or markers.
6. Glue the seeds in the box next to the flower.
7. Continue with the other two seed pockets and pictured flowers.

Going Further

In the fall, take a walk in a garden that has plants that have "gone to seed." Point out to the children the various seed pockets of the different plants. Discuss the color, size, and shape of the pockets. Then let the children open some pockets from different plants and compare the seeds. Bring some seeds back to the classroom to plant.

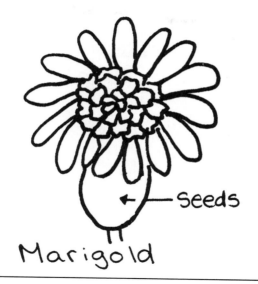

Marigold

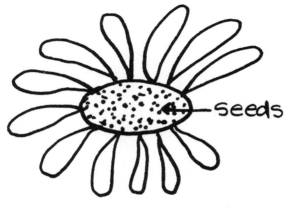

Daisy

Impatien

Activity I-B2. Cucumber Seeds

Materials Needed

- cucumber
- paper towel
- plastic serrated knife
- magnifying glass
- copy of "Cucumber Seeds" worksheet
- glue
- crayons or markers

Directions for Children

1. Cut across the cucumber in a few places and look at the seeds.
2. Pick out some of the seeds and put them on the paper towel.
3. Look at the seeds with the magnifying glass.
4. With the plastic knife, cut a bite-sized piece of the white part of the cucumber and taste it.
5. Let the seeds on the paper towel dry on a sunny windowsill.
6. With a marker or crayon, color the skin of the cucumber on the worksheet. Leave the inside of the cucumber white.
7. Glue some of the dried cucumber seeds onto the middle of the cucumber on the worksheet.
8. Take home some seeds to plant in the yard or in a cup for a windowsill.

Going Further

What Is a Seed? To explain and demonstrate the answer to this question, first soak some lima beans overnight. Show the children how to peel off a bean's outer protective covering, and carefully separate the two halves of the bean. Can the children see the tiny plant inside? Explain that the small stem will grow downward to become the beginning of the plant's roots and, at the other end of the bean, a small bud will grow upward to become the stem and leaves. The two halves of the bean are the food the plant uses until it is able to get its own food in the ground.

Now let the children peel their own lima bean seeds and discover the tiny young plant for themselves.

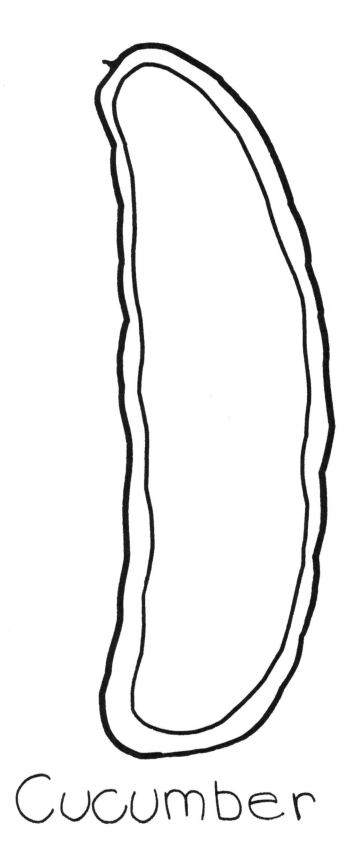

Cucumber

Activity I-B3. Tree Seeds

Materials Needed

- copy of "Tree Seeds" worksheet
- collection of acorns, polinoses, beech seed bales, and mimosa tree pods from around the school and home (look at the trees from which they have fallen)
- four small boxes (fast-food hamburger or hot dog boxes are great)
- glue
- safety scissors

Directions for Children

1. Look at the tree seeds on the worksheet.
2. Cut apart the four seed pictures and glue them to the tops of the small boxes.
3. Sort the tree seeds into the boxes.

Going Further

1. Plant a few of each kind of tree seeds in some soft ground in the schoolyard. Watch for sprouts!

2. Place several familiar leaf types, such as maple, oak, white birch, etc., on the glass plate of an overhead projector. Have the children name the types of leaves projected onto the screen.

3. *How Seeds Travel*: Explain that if all seeds fell to the ground directly beneath the parent plant, they would be so crowded for light, air, and root room that most of the plants would die. But plants have many ways of making sure that this would not happen. Some seeds travel on the wind. These kinds either have little fine broad wings—like pine seeds and maple seeds—or they are tufts that sail easily—such as silky milkweed seeds or downy dandelions.

• Let the children experiment by dropping some maple seeds (polinoses) from aloft or holding a dandelion that's gone to seed in front of a small fan. (Make sure the fan has a proper safety guard.)

• When the brittle tumbleweed breaks off, the wind blows it "head over heels" across the field. As it somersaults, it releases a few seeds at a time. It usually takes a few weeks of travel to spread all the seeds. (If a tumbleweed is not available, use a ping-pong ball to demonstrate the somersaulting of the tumbleweed.)

• Many plants that grow their seeds in pods twist open or explode to send their seeds flying through the air. Gather some pods from mimosa trees, mustard plants, or impatiens for the children to feel and open.

• Some plants produce seeds inside containers that have "hooks" or "spines" that hook onto animals and "hitch" rides for miles! The oak tree has a special friend (the squirrel) who does a lot of planting of its seed (the acorn) for it.

4. Read *The Giving Tree* by Shel Silverstein (or any other favorite book about trees). Discuss trees, how they grow, and what they need to stay alive. Have one of the children draw a tree on a large sheet of paper, showing the tree's roots going down into the soil. Explain how the roots draw water from the ground to feed the branches and leaves. This movement of water up through the tree is called "capillary action."

5. Have the children help you with this experiment: Roll several sheets of paper toweling into the shape of a stick and tape it closed. Put about two inches of water in a tall glass. Mix in a few drops of red, blue, or green food coloring. Put one end of the paper towel stick into the water. Watch as the stick draws up the water. In a few hours, the entire "stick" will be wet.

You and the children can also do some experiments with a stalk of celery instead of the paper towel stick.

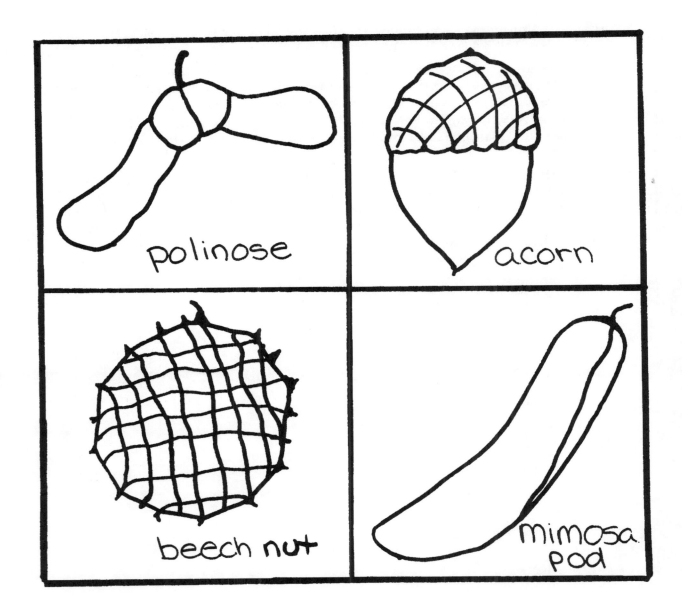

polinose

acorn

beech nut

mimosa pod

Activity I-B4. Gift Plant

Materials Needed

- cleaned tuna can or other suitable small planting container
- soil
- marigold seeds
- pencil
- 1¼" × 12" strip of paper
- tape
- markers or crayons
- moist sponge

Directions for Children

1. Decorate the paper strip with flowers, sun rays, lines, or dots.
2. Fill the can with soil and pat it down.
3. Make three holes in the soil with a pencil.
4. Drop a seed into each hole.
5. With your finger, gently cover the seeds with soil.
6. Water the seeds lightly by squeezing a moist sponge over the planted seeds.
7. Tape the decorated paper strip around the can.
8. Place the can on a sunny windowsill. Water it when the soil is dry and watch for the flowers to grow.

Going Further

Once the flowers have begun to grow, the children can give them as gifts to their family and friends.

Activity I-B5. Roots and Sprouts

Materials Needed

- copy of "Roots and Sprouts" worksheet
- commercially prepared root garden or a clear plastic glass
- markers
- crayons
- potting soil
- lima beans in water

Directions for Children

1. Soak lima beans overnight in water.

2. Fill the root garden or glass with potting soil.

3. Slide two or three lima beans down the edge of the glass so that they can be seen from the outside.

4. Observe the following:
    - the downward growth of the root
    - the upward growth of a sprout
    - the development of the root system

5. Color the seed on the worksheet.

6. When the roots on the real lima beans start growing downward, draw in roots on the worksheet with a different color.

7. When the sprout appears, draw that on the worksheet with another color.

8. Select a color to lightly go over the part of your picture that is the soil.

9. Color each part of the tablecloth with different colors.

Going Further

During the recording process, encourage the children to note that they are "acting as scientists" by observing and recording information in picture form.

Activity I-B6. Growing Sequence

Materials Needed

- copy of "Growing Sequence" worksheet
- crayons
- scissors

Note to Teacher

This activity should be done after the children observe the actual growth of roots and sprouts from a real seed. (See Activity I-B5.)

Directions for Children

1. Look at the worksheet. You are going to show how the seed grows.
2. Color all the seeds.
3. Lightly color the soil in each picture.
4. In box 2, use a crayon to draw the roots that are beginning to grow. Use another crayon to color the water drops.
5. In box 3, color the sun and then add more roots. Draw the sprout coming out of the seed.
6. In box 4, add more roots and use your crayon to draw more leaves as the sprout grows into a seedling.

Going Further

Have the children cut apart the four pictures on the lines and mix them up. Ask the children to line up the pictures in "growing order" from left to right. Discuss the order so that the children can verbalize the action that is taking place.

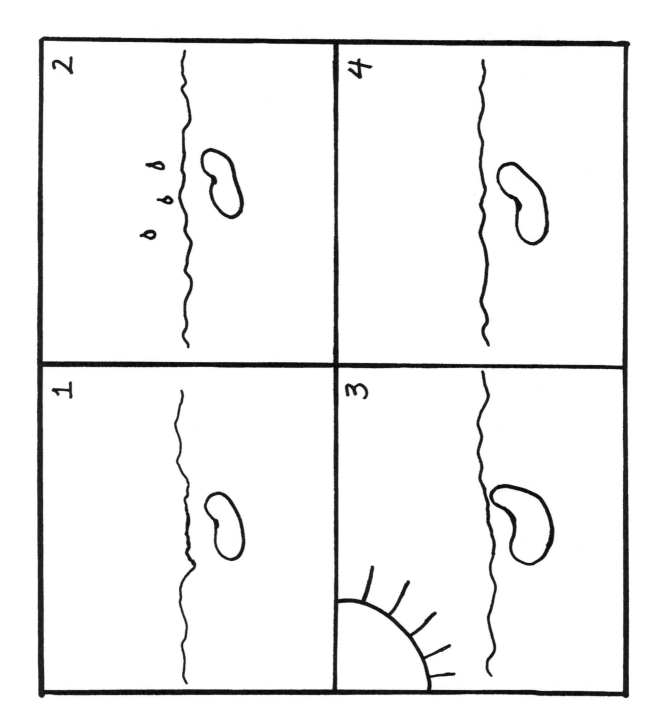

Activity I-B7. Vegetable and Flower Seed Collage

Materials Needed

- seed, vegetable, and flower catalogs
- variety of seeds
- sheet of white construction paper
- glue
- safety scissors

Directions for Children

1. Glue a border of seeds around the edge of the construction paper.

2. Cut out a variety of pictures of seeds, flowers, and vegetables from the catalogs and glue them onto the construction paper.

Going Further

1. Here's a little ditty for the children to learn, sung to the tune of "I'm a Little Teapot."

> I'm a little seed
>   short and stout.
> Plant me in the ground   (*child crouches down*)
> And I'll grow a sprout!   (*child raises one arm in air*)

2. Draw a huge seed on a large sheet of brown kraft paper. Let each child take turns drawing a root coming out of the seed. After each child has had a chance to draw a root, you can draw a sprout. Ask each child to then draw a leaf on the sprout. Label it "We Are Learning About Seeds" and display it in the hallway. (Discuss the process of growth as the children are doing the actual drawing so that they make the connection between their seed experiences and their drawing.)

3. To show the children that some seeds make nutritious snacks, roast and eat some pumpkin, sunflower, or raw peanut seeds.

4. Look up "peanuts" in a children's encyclopedia and read to the children all the many uses Dr. George Washington Carver discovered for the peanut. Make peanut butter in a blender (shelled peanuts and a little oil for smoothness). Enjoy this peanut butter on crackers as a snack with milk or juice.

I-C. AIR AND WATER

Purpose

Air and water are basics of life from which children can learn a great deal.

Although air cannot be seen, it influences our lives in very dramatic ways. In this section of the "Nature and Science Discovery Center," the children will experience air as they breathe, as the force that moves objects, and as bubbly bubbles.

The children will also experience the varied properties of water. They will be feeling water, doing sink/float experiments, measuring, and having lots of hands-on learning fun with water.

Getting Started

Have the children take a deep breath, hold it, then exhale. Discuss with the children how it feels to fill your lungs with air. Blow air into a balloon to mimic an exhale. Have the children make their breath come out of their nose by keeping their mouth closed. Have them put their hands up to their noses and mouths to feel the invisible air.

Water needs little introduction as playing and creating with water is of high interest to preschoolers. Some simple demonstrations using water with a funnel and bottles, blowing bubbles, or water painting will certainly peak their excitement to "jump right in" to these activities. Be sure to solicit from the children the many ways we use water: watering plants; making tea, coffee, hot chocolate, powdered fruit drinks; filling swimming pools; making ice cubes; taking baths; washing clothes and dishes; filling fish tanks; watering the lawn and garden; and so on.

Have the children look through old magazines for pictures of people using water in these and other ways. Make a chart of these pictures.

AIR

When demonstrating activities using drinking straws, talk to the children about blowing out, instead of sucking in.

Activity I-C1. Air Power

Materials Needed

- one of each in a small box: drinking straw, cottonball, feather, small rock, penny, one half of a tissue, eraser, small piece of wadded paper

Directions for Children

1. Take one item out of the box and put it on the table.

2. Take the drinking straw and point it at the object.

3. Blow through the straw and try to make the object move.

4. Do the same with all the other objects in the box.

5. Now repeat the experiment, only this time make two piles of the objects you have tried to blow. One pile will contain those objects that *could* be moved with the air coming out of the straw, and the other pile will contain objects that *could not* be moved.

Going Further

Have a balloon for each child. Print each child's name on a balloon with a permanent marker and give each child his or her balloon. Show an uninflated balloon to the class. Explain that they are going to fill the balloon with air and that the air will push out the sides of the balloon to make the balloon get bigger. Have each child blow up the balloon and show them how their names "grew." (Be prepared to help any child who is not able to inflate the balloon.) Let go of the balloon and have the child whose name is on the balloon try to catch it.

Activity I-C2. Little and Big Air with Soap Bubbles

Materials Needed

*   two drinking straws (one skinny and one fat)
*   plastic bowl filled with water
*   liquid dish detergent

Directions for Children

1. Take the skinny straw, put it into the bowl of water, and blow some bubbles. Notice the size of the bubbles.

2. Now take the fat straw and blow some more bubbles in the bowl of water. Notice how the fat straw makes bigger bubbles.

3. Put a drop of liquid detergent into the bowl of water.

4. Take the skinny straw and blow some bubbles in the water. Look at how many more bubbles you can make now that you have the liquid soap in your water.

5. Use the fat straw to blow bubbles in the water. See again how the fat straw makes bigger bubbles.

Going Further

1. Just for fun, add a drop of food coloring to the bowl of water with the liquid soap and stir it in. Now let the children blow their bubbles. Don't they look pretty? Try using an egg beater to make mountains of bubbles!

2. *Air Bubbles*: Explain to the children that air can be pushed from your mouth down through a straw. Have the children blow into a drinking straw and use their hand to feel the air coming out the end of the straw. (Emphasize blowing *out*, not sucking *in*.) Have the children experiment with straws of different thicknesses. Let them blow into a bowl of water and observe the different size bubbles they produce as the air pushes into the water. Ask the children to try and guess (and explain) why the fatter straw makes bigger bubbles. (The fatter straw allows more air to enter the water at one time, making a bigger bubble.)

Activity I-C3. Make a Windsock

Materials Needed

- copy of "Make a Windsock" worksheet
- six strips of colored tissue paper
- 5″ × 12″ strip of construction paper
- glue
- safety scissors
- markers or crayons
- 12″ piece of yarn
- hole puncher

Note to Teacher

Before doing this activity, be sure to introduce and explain windsocks to the children. You might want to observe one at a nearby flagpole or ask children to volunteer bringing windsocks to school. Use a fan to demonstrate how they move in the wind.

Directions for Children

1. Look at the pictures on the worksheet. They are all things that wind (air that moves quickly) moves.
2. Color all the objects and cut them out.
3. Glue the colored objects onto the strip of construction paper.
4. Then glue the ends of the construction paper together.
5. Glue the six tissue paper streamers to the construction paper.
6. Use the hole puncher to make two holes opposite each other on the construction paper.
7. String and tie the yarn to make a handle for your windsock.
8. Take your windsock outside on a windy day and watch what happens.

Going Further

Pretend to Be Birds Flying Through the Air: Point out any birds that you see in the schoolyard. Notice the different ways each kind of bird flies. Some flap their wings often, while others glide almost effortlessly. Tell the children to pretend to be birds flying through the air. Attach short crepe paper streamers to their wrists, and send them off to flap their "wings" and glide around the schoolyard. You might want to play *Peter Pan*'s "I Can Fly" song or *Jonathan Livingston Seagull*'s "Skybird."

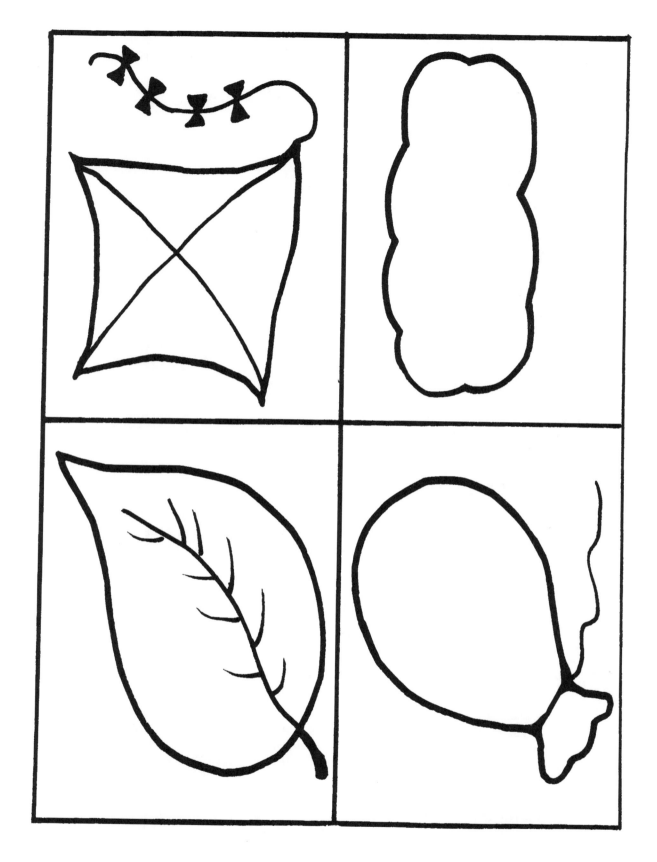

Activity I-C4. Your Wind

Materials Needed

- drinking straw
- piece of fingerpainting paper or other shiny-surfaced paper (tracing paper taped to newspaper also works well)
- watered-down tempera paint
- plastic spoon
- smock for painting

Directions for Children

1. Put on your smock.
2. Using the plastic spoon, scoop up a spoonful of paint and make a number of small paint puddles on your paper.
3. Take your straw and blow air slowly through the straw to make the paint move.
4. Blow all the puddles to make a wind design that covers your paper.
5. Observe that the harder you blow, the faster and farther the paint moves.

Going Further

Have the children make a series of these wind paintings and display them around the classroom. Can the children think of appropriate titles for the paintings? Print their suggestions on paper and place them underneath each painting.

WATER
Activity I-C5. Feeling Water

Materials Needed

- water table or basin of water
- several different sizes of plastic bottles with holes punched in them
- plastic bottle with a pump (from hand cream, shampoo, liquid soap, etc.)
- plastic strainer
- plastic funnel
- plastic spray bottle
- plastic cup

Directions for Children

1. Put your hands in the water and move them through the water. Let the water run between your fingers. Try to grab a handful. Move one hand around and around in a circle to make the water swirl; then stop and feel the rush of water against your hand.

2. Now experiment with the "feel" of the water using all your plastic objects.

3. Notice how soft the water feels when it comes out of the spray bottle; how it feels like rain when it comes through the strainer or the bottle with the holes punched in it. Feel the rush of the water as it passes through the funnel. Which way do you like best?

Going Further

1. Add a set of small plastic boats to the water table or basin. Let the children experiment by moving them with a push of water from their hand. Can they make a boat go from one side of the water table or basin to the other side without touching it?

2. Can the children make the boat move by blowing it?

Activity I-C6. Colored Water Design

Materials Needed

- two small bowls of water
- red and blue food colorings
- piece of paper toweling taped to newspaper
- two small chubby paintbrushes
- two plastic spoons
- smock for painting

Directions for Children

1. Put on the smock.

2. Put two drops of the red food coloring in one of the bowls. Watch it spread into the water. Stir the water with a spoon and observe how all the water turns the same color.

3. Now put two drops of the blue food coloring into the other bowl of water. Watch it spread into the water. Stir the water with the other spoon and watch how all the water turns the same color.

4. Take a paintbrush and dip it into one of the bowls of water. Paint some lines and dots on the paper towel.

5. Now do the same with the other brush and the other bowl of colored water.

6. Go over some of your first color lines with the second color. Does it make a new color? (Encourage the children to discuss the results, thus facilitating their language development through science exploration.)

Going Further

Bring in some ice cubes. Talk about how ice cubes are made and what we use them for. Let each child handle an ice cube. Then put several ice cubes on saucers and place them in different areas of your classroom, e.g., on a sunny windowsill, near a radiator, in a shady spot. Periodically during the next few minutes, have the children observe the melting of the cubes. Discuss what heat does to the ice cubes.

Activity I-C7. Sink or Float

Materials Needed

- water table or basin of water
- large plastic bowl filled with a selection of the following: small magnet, penny, nickle, balloon filled with water and tied, crayon, sponge, ping-pong ball, plastic boat, small empty plastic bottle (capped), plastic spoon, cork, small wooden block, and any other small sink/float items you have available

Directions for Children

1. Let's experiment. Take one item at a time out of the bowl and set it on the surface of the water.

2. Will it sink or float? Did it do what you thought it would?

3. Continue with all the items in your bowl.

4. When you have finished testing each item to see if it sinks or floats in water, take another look at the items that are floating.

5. Take them out one at a time and put them back in the bowl.

6. Now look at the items that are on the bottom of the water table.

7. Take them out one at a time and put them back in the bowl.

8. What can you say about the items that *did* float and those that *did not* float? (weight, size, and so on)

Activity I-C8. Wax Crayon Repels Water

Materials Needed

- copy of "Crayon Repels Water" worksheet
- crayons
- small bowl of water
- paintbrush
- blue tempera paint
- plastic spoon

Directions for Children

1. Color the duck on the worksheet with a crayon. Press the crayon firmly and cover the duck completely.
2. Color the lily pads with a different crayon.
3. Put a spoonful of blue tempera paint into the bowl of water and stir it.
4. Lightly paint over the *entire* picture with the blue water, including going over the duck and lily pads. Don't scrub your brush against the paper.
5. Notice how the water moves away from the crayon. There is wax in crayons and water does not stick to wax.

Going Further

Dip a candle into a glass of water. Notice how the water runs off the candle. Ask the children what they think the candle is made from. Dip a crayon in the water and observe how the water runs off the crayon just like it runs off the candle.

Activity I-C9. Measuring with Water

Materials Needed

- water table or basin of water
- selection of small- and medium-sized plastic bottles
- different-sized plastic cups
- funnel

Directions for Children

1. Fill one of the small bottles with water.
2. Put the funnel in one of the larger bottles.
3. Pour the water from the small bottle into the funnel. Does the water fill the bigger bottle?

4. Fill the little bottle again and pour it into the funnel.

5. Is the big bottle full now?

6. Do other experiments with water, bottles, cups, and the funnel. How many little bottles can you fill with one cup of water? Experiment.

Going Further

You Be the Scale: Let a child fill two children's sand pails with different amounts of water. Let a child hold one pail in each hand. Which pail is heavier? Which pail is lighter? Look in the pail. Which pail has more water in it? Which has less water in it? Continue with:

- different amounts of sand in each pail
- equal amounts of sand; however, make one bucket's sand wet and the other dry
- one bucket of sand and one bucket of water
- one bucket of sand and one bucket of pebbles
- one bucket of leaves and one bucket of twigs

Activity I-C10. We Need Water

Materials Needed

- drawing paper
- markers or crayons
- safety scissors
- sheet of construction paper
- glue

Directions for Children

1. Use markers or crayons to draw and color four pictures of things that need water to live and grow.

2. Then cut out your four pictures.

3. At the top of the construction paper, print the words WE NEED WATER.

4. Glue your four pictures onto the construction paper.

Going Further

Do an experiment with two like plants or sprouts by watering one regularly and depriving the other of water. Then have the children take note of the differences between the two plants. Discuss the changes in the plant that was deprived of water (stopped growing, leaves turned yellow, wilted, and so on).

I-D. ANIMALS AND PETS

Purpose

The children will learn what some animals do to survive during the winter months when food is scarce. They will also become more familiar with the variety of pets that people can have.

Getting Started

1. Invite a pet store owner, a local veterinarian, or an animal shelter volunteer to visit the classroom and talk to the children about different animals. If the visitor is able to bring actual animals, the presentation would be even more exciting!

2. Read *Millions of Cats* by Wanda Gag or *So Many Cats* by Beatrice Schenk de Regniers. Have the children dramatize the different ways various animals move:

   - slither like a snake
   - waddle like a duck
   - crawl like a turtle
   - hop like a bunny
   - swim like a fish
   - fly like a bird

Activity I-D1. Bear's Long Sleep

Materials Needed

- copy of "Bear's Long Sleep" worksheet (two pages)
- crayons
- safety scissors
- four paper fasteners

Note to Teacher

Explain to the children that in the winter bears cannot find food to eat. There are no berries on the bushes; the fish in the lakes are at the bottom of the water so that they don't freeze at the top of the lakes and ponds; and there are no insects to be found and no honey to get from the bees. So, bears curl up in a cave and sleep until spring arrives.

Directions for Children

1. Use crayons to lightly color the bear's body, arms, and legs on the two worksheet pages.

2. Cut out the pieces.

3. Attach the arms and the legs to the body with paper fasteners at the X's.

4. Make your bear curl up for its long winter's nap by moving its arms and legs up and around its body and head.

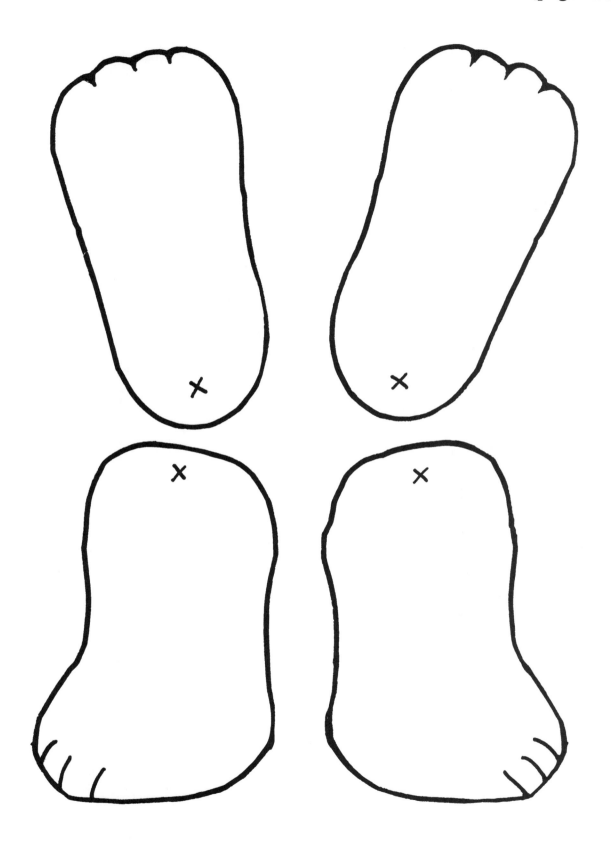

Activity I-D2. Snowshoe Rabbit

Materials Needed

- copy of "Snowshoe Rabbit" worksheet
- brown crayon
- craft stick
- glue
- safety scissors

Note to Teacher

Explain to the children that snowshoe rabbits have long and broad feet so that they can hop on top of deep snow. (Show a picture of the snowshoes that people can wear to walk on snow.) The fur of the snowshoe rabbit gradually changes from brown in the summer to white in the winter so that the rabbit can blend in with its seasonal environment and thus hide from other animals.

Directions for Children

1. Draw a face on the snowshoe rabbit. Then color the rabbit with the brown crayon.
2. Cut out the snowshoe rabbit.
3. Draw a face on the white side of the rabbit. Your teacher can print WINTER on this side of the rabbit.
4. Glue the snowshoe rabbit to the craft stick.

Going Further

Declare "It's winter!" Everyone must turn their craft sticks to show the white rabbit and hop. Then, "It's summer!" Everyone switches to the brown rabbit and hops.

SUMMER

Activity I-D3. Shhh! They're Sleeping

Materials Needed

- copy of "Shhh! They're Sleeping" worksheet
- crayons or markers
- 9″ × 12″ brown construction paper
- cotton balls
- glue

Note to Teacher

Explain to the children that in the winter, when it is very cold, some small animals look for a place that is warm to sleep until spring (hibernate). Small animals—like turtles, snakes, and mice—burrow under the ground, under logs, or under rocks to escape the ice, snow, and lack of a food supply.

Directions for Children

1. With crayons or markers, lightly color the animals on the worksheet.

2. Cut the piece of construction paper as shown here.

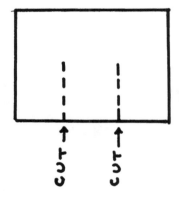

3. Glue the top of the construction paper onto the worksheet as shown here.

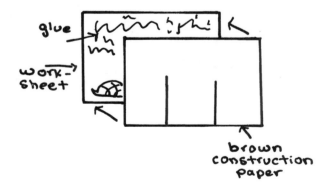

4. Pull apart the cotton balls and glue them to the brown construction paper as "handles" on the three "doors."

5. Say "Shhh" as you pick up each construction paper "door" to see who is "hibernating" beneath it.

Going Further

Play "Sleeping Mice." Have three or four children curl up on the carpet and pretend to be sleeping. Designate one child to be "Spring." The rest of the class holds hands in a circle around the "sleepers." Have the children sing the following as they slowly walk around:

> Shhh! Shhh! They are all sleeping.
> It's winter, too cold to be creeping.
> Wait! Wait! Spring will be coming,
> Then they can rise and start their running.

Have the child designated as "Spring" touch the shoulder of one of the sleeping mice and announce "It's Spring!" This mouse "wakes up," runs around the other mice, and then joins the circle. Repeat the sound and touch until all the mice are awake and in the circle.

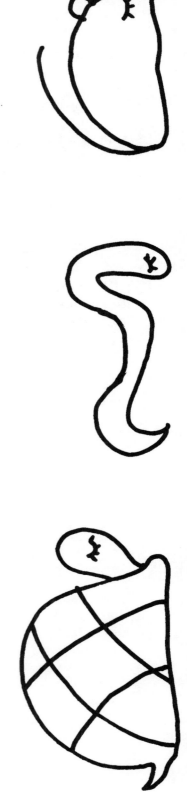

Activity I-D4. Paper Plate Turtle

Materials Needed

- copy of "Paper Plate Turtle" worksheet
- crayons or markers
- safety scissors
- six paper fasteners
- hole puncher
- paper plate

Directions for Children

1. Select a color for your paper plate turtle.

2. Your teacher can help you punch six holes around the paper plate as shown on the worksheet.

3. Color all the parts of the turtle on the worksheet.

4. Cut out all of the turtle's parts and attach them to the paper plate with the paper fasteners.

Going Further

1. Teach the children this poem, using their paper plate turtle for the movements:

This is my turtle.	*(hold up turtle)*
He lives in a shell.	*(turn in all parts to hide)*
He likes his home very well.	
He pokes his head out when he wants to eat.	*(move out head)*
He pulls his head back when he wants to sleep.	*(move head back behind shell)*
Good night, little turtle!	

2. Read *I Love My Pet* by Anne and Harlow Rockwell. Ask the children what kinds of pets they have at home. (If some children do not have any pets, ask them what kinds of pets they would like to have.) Begin a discussion about pets by asking about size, color, sleeping and eating habits. Discuss the kind of care that each animal needs. Show pictures of household pets. If possible, bring in a live pet and invite the children to discuss the animal and gently pet it (if applicable). If a dog is brought in, be sure to read *Harry the Dirty Dog* by Gene Zion or some of the many "Clifford" books by Norman Bridwell.

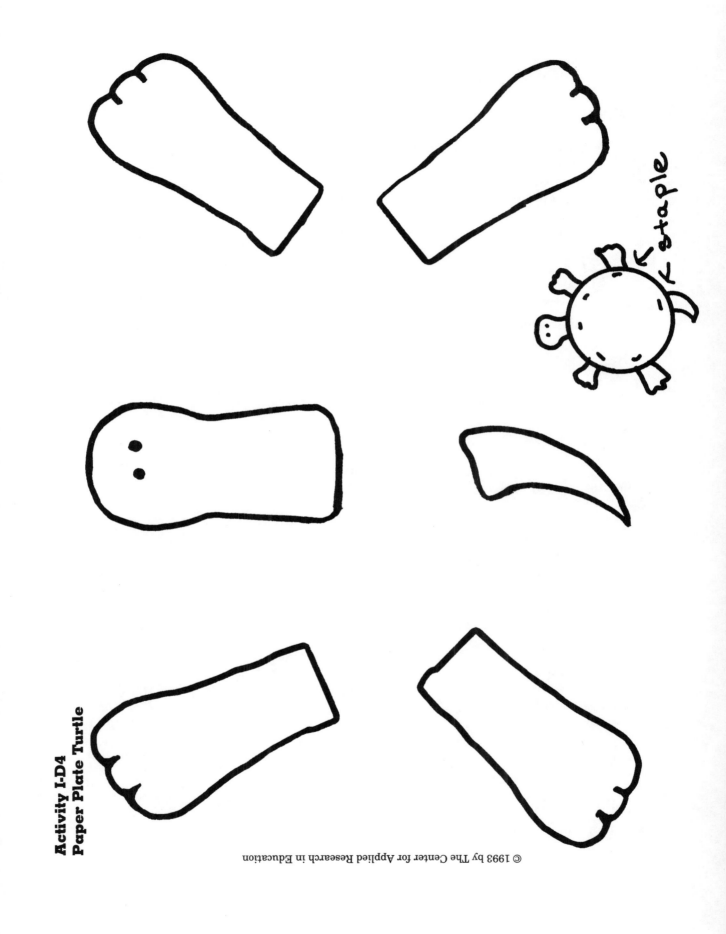

Activity I-D4
Paper Plate Turtle

staple

II. Creative Arts Discovery Center

All children are natural artists—their creative instincts are innate and their experiments with various art media are refreshingly uninhibited. Since art is a nonverbal means of communication, the children's creations will be as spontaneous and special as they are. In the Creative Arts Discovery Center, children are provided with many opportunities to experiment with various art materials, to learn about their qualities, and to discover what makes them special.

Creative Arts Discovery Center
Management Sheet

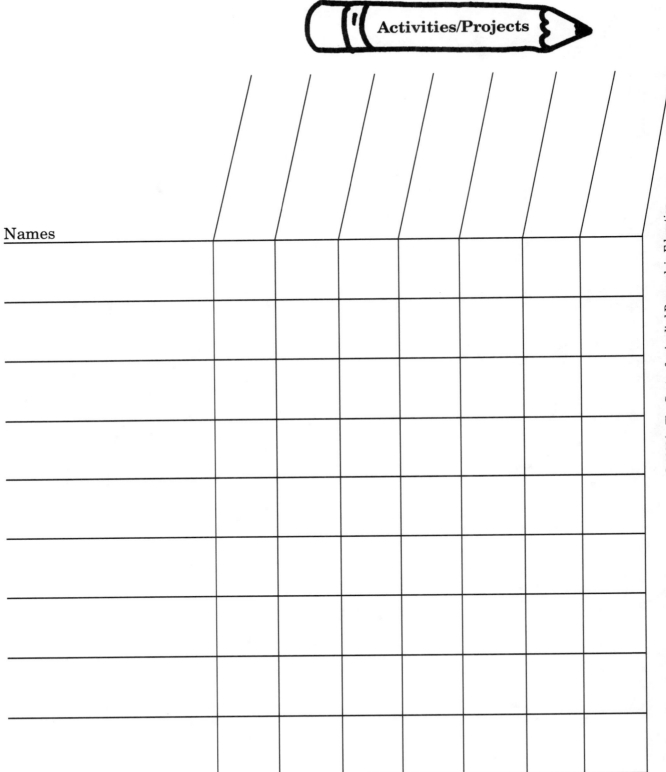

Activities/Projects

Names

Creative Arts Discovery Center Management Sheet

Activities/Projects

Names

II-A. DESIGN

Purpose

Creating free-form designs will give children the opportunity to explore each art medium's qualities to its fullest. The free movement of the artist's hand across the paper will create a unique art experience for the child and an equally unique "work of art."

Getting Started

1. Let the children listen to you briefly describe your personal feelings and sensations when using various art mediums and supplies. When you express the feel of your fingers moving the cool finger paint around the slippery paper or tell how it feels to create a collage by gluing materials where you think they would look best, the children are motivated to eagerly engage in the magic of creative art.

2. During that time of your preschool day when you explain the Center's activities, allow the children to experiment with the materials as much as possible and to find their own creative paths.

Activity II-A1. Wet Chalk Art

Materials Needed

- finger-painting paper taped to newspaper
- colored chalk
- small cup of water
- small piece of sponge
- art smock

Note to Teacher

To prevent the finished wet chalk drawings from smearing, you may want to spray them with a fixative before displaying. Be sure to follow the directions on the fixative and to spray in a well-ventilated area.

Directions for Children

1. Dip the sponge in the cup of water and wet the paper.
2. Choose a piece of colored chalk and make a design on the paper.

3. Choose a different color chalk and continue with the design.

4. Continue as above with the other colors.

5. Let your design dry into a bright creation.

Going Further

1. The smooth easy strokes that the children make with their wet chalk lend themselves to creating designs to music. Have the children listen to a cassette or record of flowing music, such as "The Waltz of the Flowers," while creating their designs. Or you might try a fast-paced tune like "The March of the Wooden Soldiers."

2. Have the children use light-colored chalk dipped in water to make a design on a piece of black construction paper. The contrasting colors make a dramatic presentation. The children might also use white chalk dipped in water to make Halloween ghosts on black or orange construction paper.

Activity II-A2. Sponge Paint Design

Materials Needed

- three small pieces of sponge
- three small paper cups or margarine lids
- yellow, red, and blue tempera paints
- construction paper
- art smock
- newspaper to cover work area

Directions for Children

1. Pour a small amount of different tempera paint into each cup.

2. Place the end of each piece of sponge into a different cup.

3. Choose a color to begin with. Dab the sponge up and down in any pattern (or no pattern) all over the construction paper.

4. Do the same with the other two colors.

5. Notice how the overlapping of any two colors will create a new color, such as: yellow and blue make green; red and yellow make orange; blue and red make purple.

Going Further

Make a sponge-painted rainbow. Have the children start by dipping a sponge in paint and sliding it in an arc on a sheet of construction paper. Then they make an arc of another color under the first arc; then another colored arc under the second arc.

Activity II-A3. Spoon Paint

Materials Needed

- three small paper cups
- red, yellow, and blue tempera paints
- construction paper
- three plastic spoons
- newspapers
- art smock

Directions for Children

1. Cover your work surface with newspaper.
2. Pour a small amount of different paint into the three cups.
3. Fold a piece of construction paper in half and then open it up.
4. Spoon small amounts of paint onto one half of the construction paper.
5. Close the other half of the paper on top of the paint.
6. Press down on this part of the paper. Rub your hand all around the paper.
7. Open the paper to see your beautiful spoon-paint design.
8. What does your design look like to you? Tell about it.

Going Further

Make a monarch butterfly. The children will need a small cup of orange tempera paint, a cup of black tempera paint, two plastic spoons, and a sheet of white construction paper folded in half. Have the children open the construction paper and spoon small amounts of each of the colors onto one half of the construction paper. They then close the paper and move their hands all around on the top of the closed paper. Ask them to open the paper to see a striking monarch butterfly!

Activity II-A4. Ink Spots

Materials Needed

- three or four layers of newspapers
- small cup of water
- small piece of sponge
- two colors of ink
- pens for ink
- tape
- finger-paint paper
- art smock

Directions for Children

1. Tape your paper to the newspapers.
2. Wet your paper with the sponge and water.
3. Carefully dip a pen in the ink and touch it to the wet paper.
4. Watch the ink move in the water.
5. Repeat in other places on your paper.
6. Do the same with the other color of ink. What is happening? Why?

Going Further

Have the children make wrapping paper. They will need a sheet of white tissue paper, colored inks, and cotton swabs. Lay out the tissue paper on a piece of newspaper. Dip a cotton swab in one of the colored inks, and then touch the swab to the tissue paper. Watch the ink spread through the fibers of the tissue paper. Have the children continue to make dots all over the paper. They can repeat the process with the other colors.

Activity II-A5. Fingerprints

Materials Needed

- two different colored ink pads
- construction paper

Directions for Children

1. Press your finger or fingers onto one of the ink pads and then onto the construction paper.

2. Repeat this procedure all over your paper.

3. Use your other hand and the other ink pad to add more fingerprints to your paper.

Going Further

1. Make a picture of yourself with your fingerprints. There's nothing more "you" than your fingerprint!

2. What else can the children create with their fingerprints—a house? a flower? a bunny?

3. Have the children compare two different fingerprints, perhaps yours and a child's. Use a magnifying glass to see the details clearly.

Activity II-A6. Straw Painting

Materials Needed

- two small straws cut in half
- four small paper cups
- four colors of tempera paint
- water
- construction paper
- art smocks
- newspapers to cover work area

Directions for Children

1. In a cup, mix a drop of tempera paint with about one-half inch of water.
2. Dip one end of a straw into the paint wash.
3. Put your index finger on the top of the straw.
4. Carefully move the straw to your construction paper.
5. Take your finger off the end of the straw. What happens?
6. Repeat with the other colors.

Going Further

1. Let the children put a spoonful of the tempera and water mix on a piece of finger-painting paper. With a short straw, they then blow the mix around the paper. (Be sure the children don't try to "drink" the paint.)

2. Instead of blowing the mix around the paper, have the children drag it by putting the straw (or a cotton swab) into the mixture and moving it around the paper.

Activity II-A7. Crayon Resist

Materials Needed

- crayons
- construction paper
- wash of ½ teaspoon tempera paint (any color) and ½ cup of water
- stubby paintbrush

Directions for Children

1. Use your crayons to make a design on your construction paper.
2. Paint over your crayon design with your tempera paint wash.
3. Watch how the paint wash moves away from the crayon. Do you know why this might happen?

Going Further

Make some stars at night! Have the children tape a piece of white ditto paper onto some newspaper, and then make a design of stars with a silver or white crayon. With a wash of one-half teaspoon black tempera paint and a half cup of water, the children paint over their entire paper. See how the stars shine at night!

Activity II-A8. Glue and Wash

Materials Needed

- small (1¼-ounces) container of white glue
- construction paper
- wash of ½ teaspoon tempera paint (any color) and ½ cup of water
- paintbrush
- newspapers to cover work area
- art smock

Directions for Children

1. With your glue, make a line design on your construction paper.
2. Let it dry completely.

3. Brush over your glue design with the tempera wash.

4. Notice how the wash fills in the spaces between your glue lines.

Going Further

1. Elmer's® Glue-All also comes in fluorescent colors! You might want to try these colors instead of the white.

2. For holiday fun, have the children trace a shamrock, draw a heart, a Christmas tree, a Star of David, or a bunny on their construction paper. Go over the lines with glue and let the glue dry. The children paint over the shape with the tempera wash.

Activity II-A9. Paper Towel Design

Materials Needed

- red and yellow finger paints (or any other two colors)
- white construction paper
- paper towels
- newspapers
- tape
- art smock

Directions for Children

1. Tape the white construction paper to the newspaper.
2. Put a spoonful of each color of finger paint on the construction paper.
3. Wad up a few sheets of paper toweling.
4. Dab the wad up and down in the paint and all around the construction paper. Cover the whole paper.
5. The colors will mix and blend to make a unique three-color design.

Going Further

This project is good for children to get hands-on experience in color mixing. The activity suggests red and yellow paint, so the stamping will come out red, yellow, and orange. This is a good paper towel color design to do around Halloween.

Do a blue and yellow (to make green) design around Christmas or St. Patrick's Day. Red and blue (with some white added) makes a nice lilac hue to use around Mother's Day or any time in Spring.

Use these designs to make backdrops for construction paper holiday cut-outs. Help the children write messages or greetings on the cut-outs and glue them on the paper-towel designs.

II-B. COLLAGES AND MOSAICS

Purpose

Creating collages and mosaics is a relaxing, enjoyable experience for children. These art forms are great for promoting fine-motor control, patterning, and attention to details.

An advantage for *you* is the ease of gathering the materials to create the collages and mosaics.

Activity II-B1. Snip and Glue

Materials Needed

- six-inch strips of construction paper in various colors
- scissors
- small container of white glue
- construction paper

Directions for Children

1. Use your scissors to cut the construction paper strips into small pieces. Snip the pieces at different angles.
2. Put small dots of glue all over your construction paper.
3. Lay your snips of paper on the glue spots.

Going Further

Make a rectangle or square collage. Have the children snip the construction paper strips into small rectangles or squares. They then put small drops of glue all over a sheet of construction paper and lay on the rectangles or squares.

Activity II-B2. Toy Collage

Materials Needed

- toy store flyers, catalogs, and/or newspaper ads
- scissors
- glue
- construction paper

Directions for Children

1. Cut out pictures of your favorite toys.
2. Glue the pictures all over your construction paper.

Going Further

The children can create a fruit and vegetable collage from supermarket circulars, or a sports collage from sports magazines or sports sections of newspapers.

Activity II-B3. The Moon and Stars

Materials Needed

- copy of "Moon and Stars" worksheet
- crayons or markers
- scissors
- glue
- black construction paper

Directions for Children

1. Draw a face on the moon. Then color the moon and the stars.
2. Cut the stars into strips; then into individual star squares.
3. Cut out the moon.
4. Glue the moon in the middle of your construction paper. Glue the stars all around the rest of your paper.

Going Further

Talk to the children about the different phases of the moon. You can show pictures of the phases and perhaps help the children look on a calendar for when the different phases will occur that month.

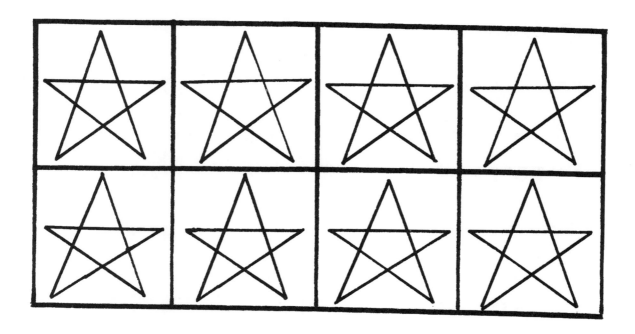

Activity II-B4. Large to Small Pile-Up

Materials Needed

- three piles of construction paper squares: 2-inch (large) squares, 1-inch (medium) squares, and ½-inch (small) squares
- glue
- construction paper

Directions for Children

1. Glue the large squares onto the construction paper. Cover as much of the paper as you can.
2. Now glue the medium squares on top of the large squares.
3. Your third level will be the small squares glued onto the medium squares.

Going Further

Have the children make a large to small pyramid. On a sheet of construction paper, the children glue a line of the largest squares across the bottom of the paper. On top of that line, they glue another line of the same-sized squares, one square less in length on each side. With their medium-sized squares, they glue two lines on top of the large squares, leaving one square off each end of the second line as they did before. The children repeat with the small squares, but continue with the small squares until they make a pyramid shape.

Activity II-B5. Mosaic Apple

Materials Needed

- copy of "Mosaic Apple" worksheet
- pile of small (approximately ½ inch) red construction paper squares
- ten small brown construction paper squares
- twenty small green construction paper squares
- glue

Directions for Children

1. Put a line of glue around the outside edge of the apple.
2. Place the red squares, one after another, on the glue.
3. Now put some glue in the middle of the apple. Lay red squares on this glue.

4. Put a line of glue on the apple's stem. Place the brown squares on the glue.

5. Put a line of glue around the edge of the apple's leaf. Place the green squares on this glue. Put glue in the center of the leaf and fill it in with the rest of your green squares.

Going Further

Make additional fruit collages by drawing simple fruit shapes on a piece of construction paper. Then have the children make them into mosaic fruits as they did the apple.

Activity II-B6. Leaf Collage

Materials Needed

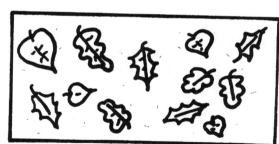

- variety of small leaves
- magazines and books
- glue
- construction paper

Directions for Children

1. Collect a variety of small leaves.
2. Press the leaves between the pages of old magazines topped with books.
3. After a few days of pressing, remove the leaves.
4. Glue the leaves all over your sheet of construction paper.

Going Further

1. To preserve and make the leaf collage shine, the children can paint over it with a glue mix of half water and half glue.

2. Let the children experiment to create a funny "Leaf Man" or "Leaf Lady." Have them glue one pressed leaf in the center of a piece of construction paper. Distribute markers or crayons—and let the children create!

Activity II-B7. Styrofoam Maze

Materials Needed

- variety of styrofoam packing shapes
- glue
- construction paper

Directions for Children

1. Put a line of glue across the top of your construction paper.
2. Lay on one kind of styrofoam packing.
3. Continue the glue and styrofoam down the sides and along the bottom of the construction paper.
4. Put a line of glue next to the top row of styrofoam. Lay on a different kind of packing.
5. Continue as above along the sides and bottom of the construction paper.

6. Do the same with the other packing shapes until you reach the center of your paper.

Going Further

Have the children make styrofoam fish. On a sheet of light blue construction paper, have the children glue three pieces of styrofoam packing (spaced apart from each other) and let dry. Treating the styrofoam as the fish's body, ask the children to use markers to add a head, fins, and a colorful tail.

Activity II-B8. Eggshell Collage

Materials Needed

- colored eggshells (see #2 in "Going Further") in red, orange, yellow, green, blue, and purple
- three plastic sandwich bags
- white glue
- marker
- construction paper
- newspaper to cover work area

Directions for Children

1. Lay the newspaper on your work area.
2. Separate the eggshells by color into three piles. You can put red and orange in one pile; yellow and green in another; and blue and purple in another.
3. Put each pile in a different plastic bag and gently crush the shells with your hand.
4. With your marker, draw two lines on your paper to divide it into four sections.
5. Spread glue in one section.
6. With your fingertips, pick up and sprinkle the crushed eggshells from one bag onto the glue. Shake off the excess onto newspaper.
7. Spread glue on another section. Pick up and sprinkle the crushed shells from another bag onto this section. Shake off the excess onto newspaper.
8. Continue with the third section.
9. Use the excess eggshells on the newspaper to fill the fourth section with this mix of the three bags.

Going Further

1. Have the children draw a large oval on their construction paper and squeeze a line of white glue on the line. Let them sprinkle the crushed eggshells on the line and then shake off the excess shells. Now ask the children to make other lines of glue—crossovers, squiggles, stripes—on the inside of the oval and sprinkle with the crushed eggshells. The children can shake off the excess and let it dry into an original mosaic egg.

2. Experiment with dying hard-boiled eggs. Let the children experiment to discover that the longer an egg is in the dye, the darker (or deeper) the color gets. Mix primary colors of dye to make secondary dye colors.

Activity II-B9. Pasta Collage

Materials Needed

- variety of uncooked pasta
  (elbows, wheels, bows, small shells)
- glue
- construction paper

Directions for Children

1. Put a drop of glue on your construction paper.
2. Place a piece of pasta on the glue.
3. Continue to fill your paper with glue and pasta.

Going Further

1. After their pasta collages have dried, let the children paint them with tempera paints.

2. Around the edge of a piece of sturdy tagboard or matboard, have the children glue pasta wheels or bows one next to each other. The children can paint the pasta frame with an appropriate holiday or seasonal color. Then let the children draw a picture or design to fit the inside of their frame, and glue it in the frame. This project makes a great gift for any occasion!

II-C. CLAY

Purpose

Clay offers a tactile experience that is hard to resist. In a child's hand, a ball of clay is an object of immeasurable possibilities. Squishing, rolling, and pounding clay give young children's fingers a marvelous fine-motor workout. With clay, children can create three-dimensional objects, patterns, designs, and shapes that are all recyclable!

Activity II-C1. Clay Nest and Eggs

Materials Needed

- clay
- clay board
- clay hammer

Directions for Children

1. Take a piece of clay about the size of a golf ball.
2. Hammer it flat with your clay hammer.
3. Bring up the sides of the clay and pinch them together to form a "nest."
4. Take small pieces of clay and roll them into balls between one palm and the clay board.
5. Put all your "eggs" in your clay nest.
6. What else might you make to go in a little clay nest?

Going Further

After making the clay nest, have the children look for pictures of birds in magazines. Then ask the children to try to make clay birds and put them in the clay nests. The children can also add some (spring) twigs (with buds and emerging leaves).

Activity II-C2. Clay Snowman

Materials Needed

- clay
- clay board
- pictures of snowmen
- cassette or record of "Frosty the Snowman"

Note to Teacher

Play the song "Frosty the Snowman" while the children are creating their snowmen.

Directions for Children

1. Look at the pictures of the snowmen and think of a snowman you may have made in the snow.
2. Use this clay to make your own standing snowman. Let's see how you figure out how to do this.

Going Further

Read the story *Frosty the Snowman*. Ask the children why they think snow melts. Then discuss the reason why Frosty melted. If snow is available, bring some indoors to make a miniature snowman and observe it melting. Have the children talk about why their clay snowmen will not melt, but how the real snowman is made of snow that melts if temperatures are above freezing.

Activity II-C3. Clay Snakes

Materials Needed

- clay
- clay board

Directions for Children

1. Take a small piece of clay and roll it back and forth on your clay board with the palm of your hand until it gets long and skinny.
2. Take another piece of clay and do the same back-and-forth rolling with your palm.
3. Look at your "snakes." Which one is longer? You can press eyes into your snakes' heads with your finger.
4. Make as many snakes as you can with your clay.
5. Pick out the longest snake and the shortest snake.

Going Further

Look up snakes in a children's encyclopedia, or get a library book about snakes. Explain that there are over 2,000 different kinds of snakes and that they live every place in the world except in the polar regions and on some of the ocean islands including Hawaii. Show the children these places on a map. Elicit from the children some ways snakes are different from air animals and other land/water animals (snakes are cold-blooded, limbless, can swallow prey larger than the width of their mouths, shed their skin).

Activity II-C4. Clay Pancake Design

Materials Needed

- clay
- clay hammer
- pencil
- comb
- acorn caps
- thread spool

Directions for Children

1. Hammer down a large piece of clay into a pancake.
2. With a pencil, make lines and dots in your pancake.
3. Press the comb into the pancake in a few places.
4. Hold the stem of an acorn cap and make some more impressions in the pancake.
5. Now with the spool, go around the edge of your pancake to make a frame for your design.

Going Further

Make believe you're preparing an Italian meal. Roll up a ball of clay, flatten it into a circle, and cut it up with a plastic knife as if it were a pizza. Or, roll up some meatballs and some skinny "snakes" to make meatballs and spaghetti. Try making Italian bread and slicing it with a plastic knife.

Activity II-C5. Gingerbread Clay Man

Materials Needed

- clay
- clay board
- pictures of gingerbread men cookies (or actual cookies)
- items for adding facial features (buttons, yarn, etc.)

Note to Teacher

You may either show pictures of gingerbread men cookies or have the children help you bake some as models.

Directions for Children

1. Look at the gingerbread men.
2. Use this clay to make your own clay gingerbread man. Let's see how you figure out how to do this.

Going Further

1. Have the children listen to or watch the story of the gingerbread man. Teach them the gingerbread man's song:

> Run, run, run as fast as you can.
> You can't catch me, I'm the gingerbread man!

Encourage the children to act out the story with their clay gingerbread men.

2. If you and the children have baked real gingerbread men cookies, now's a good time to enjoy them (with small cups of milk) as a snack.

Activity II-C6. Clay Porcupine

Materials Needed

- clay
- clay board
- pictures of a porcupine
- toothpicks

Note to Teacher

Display some pictures of porcupines and discuss this animal with the children.

Directions for Children

1. Take a large piece of clay and roll it back and forth with your hands to make a fat sausage shape.
2. Squeeze it a little about a third of the way down to make a neck and a head.
3. Take four little pieces of clay and stick them to the body to make legs.
4. With your finger, press in the eyes, a nose, and a mouth.
5. Stick toothpicks all over your porcupine's back to make its quills.
6. Think of a name for your porcupine.

Going Further

Look up porcupines in a children's encyclopedia and read to the children what porcupines do when they fear danger. Discuss their size and where they live.

II-D. TISSUE

Purpose

Working with white and colored tissue paper helps children explore the relationship between primary and secondary colors, and color intensity. It also provides fine-motor and patterning practice.

Activity II-D1. Sun-Glow Pumpkin

Materials Needed

- copy of "Pumpkin" worksheet
- 9″ × 12″ tracing paper
- 1½-inch squares of orange and yellow tissue
- glue mix of half white glue and half water in a small bowl
- paintbrush
- pencil
- newspaper and tape

Note to Teacher

In step 4, encourage the children to overlap the tissue squares. Ask them what happens when orange is placed over orange (makes a darker orange) and what happens when yellow is placed over orange (makes a lighter orange).

Directions for Children

1. With your pencil, trace the pumpkin from the worksheet onto your tracing paper.
2. Tape the tracing paper to the newspaper.
3. Paint a small section inside the pumpkin with the glue mix.
4. Lay on the tissue squares to cover the glue mix.
5. Continue until you have covered the whole pumpkin.
6. Carefully paint a light coat of the glue mix over the surface of the tissue paper. Your teacher can help you with this.
7. Let the pumpkin dry completely.

8. Cut out or tear the pumpkin on the line.

9. Hang the pumpkin in a sunny window and watch it glow!

Going Further

The children can do this same procedure with other themes, such as hearts for Valentine's Day, shamrocks for St. Patrick's Day, turkeys for Thanksgiving, and so on. Details can be added with a marker after the project has dried.

Activity II-D2. Indian Corn

Materials Needed

- copy of "Indian Corn" worksheet
- markers or crayons
- glue
- one-inch squares of red, yellow, and orange tissue paper

Directions for Children

1. Color the "leaves" (husks) of the Indian corn yellow.
2. Put a small drop of glue in one of the boxes on the corn cob.
3. Put a piece of tissue paper on the glue. This is your first "kernel."
4. Continue to cover the cob with red, yellow, and orange kernels.

Going Further

Bring in some real Indian corn for the children to feel and examine. Explain that it was the main source of food for many native American Indian tribes and how the Pilgrims (some of the first people to come over the sea to this country) were saved from starving by the corn that the Indians shared with them.

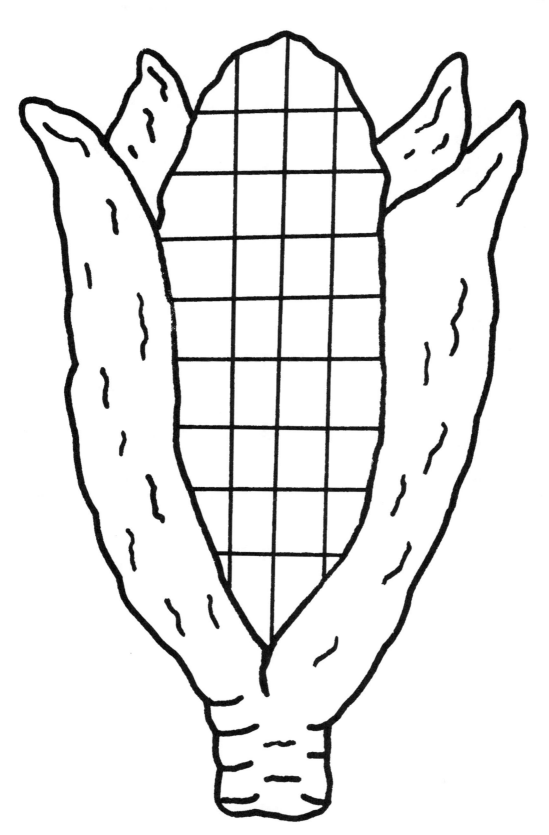

Activity II-D3. An Autumn Tree

Materials Needed

- copy of "An Autumn Tree" worksheet
- 1½-inch squares of red, yellow, and orange tissue
- glue
- markers or crayons

Note to Teacher

If you live in an area of the country where the leaves change color in the autumn, then bring the children outside for a walk around the neighborhood to look at the various colors. If the trees in your area do not change, then show pictures to the children.

Directions for Children

1. Look at the pictures of the autumn trees…OR…Think of the trees we saw outside.
2. Use this worksheet and the materials to make your own colorful autumn tree. Let's see how you figure out how to do this.

Going Further

You might want to talk with your children about how autumn leaves change color. Explain that these colors are covered by green chlorophyll in the spring and summer. In the autumn when the leaves stop making chlorophyll, the green color goes away and you can see all the beautiful colors of the leaves.

Activity II-D4. Lighter and Darker

Materials Needed

- tracing paper
- 1½-inch squares of red, white, and black tissue
- glue mix of half white glue and half water mixed in a small bowl
- paintbrush
- newspaper and tape

Directions for Children

1. Tape the tracing paper to the newspaper.
2. Paint a small section of the tracing paper with the glue mix.
3. Lay on the red tissue squares.
4. Continue to cover the tracing paper with the red tissues.
5. Paint a light coat of glue mix on the surface of the red tissue squares.
6. Now lay some white tissue squares on top of the red squares. Notice how the red looks lighter.
7. Now lay some black tissue squares on top of the red squares. Notice how the red looks darker.
8. After the project has dried, hold it up to the window to again see how white and black make colors lighter and darker.

Going Further

1. The children can further explore lighter and darker with tempera paint. Have them make two small cups of a selected color. Add white tempera to one cup and mix to make the color lighter; mix some black into the other cup to make the color darker. Observe and discuss the changes with the children.

2. Paint a lighter/darker design. Have the children draw a circle in the middle of a sheet of construction paper, and paint it with tempera paint. Then they add white to the paint and mix it in; make some lines and dots with this lighter color. Add black to the paint and mix it in to make a darker hue, and have the children make some more lines and dots on their paper. Can the children see the differences in the three hues?

Activity II-D5. My Aquarium

Materials Needed

- 12″ × 18″ white construction paper
- crayons or markers
- glue mix of half white glue and half water mixed in a small bowl
- 1½-inch squares of light blue tissue
- paintbrush
- newspapers to cover work area

Note to Teacher

If you happen to have an aquarium in the classroom (or school), let the children take time to look at it. If one is not available, perhaps you could arrange for a visit to a pet shop that has an aquarium on display. In any case, let your children become familiar with an aquarium of some kind.

Directions for Children

1. Think of the aquarium we've just seen...OR...visited.
2. Use the materials to make your own aquarium. Let's see how you figure out how to do this.

Going Further

Is there an aquarium/museum in your town or nearby? Perhaps the children might enjoy visiting and seeing some fish and other sea life up close!

III. Numbers Discovery Center

The Numbers Discovery Center gives preschoolers a strong hands-on foundation in what numbers represent. When children become comfortable with numbers—concrete counting, sorting, recognizing numerals, one-to-one correspondence, recognizing more/less, same/different—they will be better able to successfully transfer their knowledge to more abstract math. These activities also help build small-motor skills.

Numbers Discovery Center Management Sheet

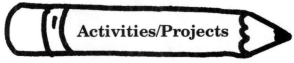
Activities/Projects

Names

Numbers Discovery Center Management Sheet

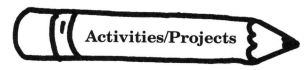
Activities/Projects

Names

III-A. COUNTING

Purpose

Concrete counting is the foundation for a successful math career. If children can internalize, through their sense of touch, what numbers mean, they can easily move on to higher levels of math skill. Through these counting activities, the children will develop a strong sense of the relationship between the quantity of objects and the number names we give them.

Getting Started

Numbers and the preschool setting go hand in hand. From the first day of school, have the children listen as you count out the straws, the milk containers, and the napkins. Direct them with such phrases as, "Only take two cookies today from the cookie basket because today's cookies are big." "Take three slices of apple, count them as you take them, then count them again after they are on your napkin." "Let's count the number of boys in the class today; the number of girls." "Who do we have more of—boys or girls?" "As I point, let's say the name of the numerals on the calendar." "Let's count how many days until Halloween."…And so on.

Note to Teacher

Although a particular skill is given for each activity, many of the activities have an overlapping of skills. A counting activity, for example, could certainly also teach numeral recognition.

Activity III-A1. Button Holes

Materials Needed

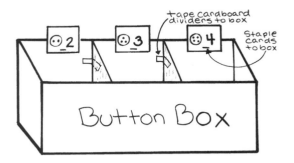

- collection of 2-hole, 3-hole, and 4-hole buttons in a small box or on a plate
- shoe box divided into three sections with three index cards labeled as shown

Directions for Children

1. Take a button and count how many holes it has.
2. Look at the shoe box numerals. Can you find the numeral that is the same

as the number of holes on your button? If not, count the dots on the cards. Then put the button in the proper part of the box.

3. Do the same with the other buttons.

Going Further

Have the children bring in any spare buttons they may have at home. Have them count as they put their buttons into a large jar. (They will love watching the volume of buttons increase!) Have five cards with a different numeral from 1 to 5 on them. Ask the children to take turns taking buttons from the jar and placing the correct numeral on each of the index cards. You can help the children glue the buttons onto the cards to make permanent counting cards.

Activity III-A2. Penny Counting

Materials Needed

- fifteen or more pennies in a cup
- five small plastic plates
- the numerals 1, 2, 3, 4, 5 each written on a half of an index card
- tape

Directions for Children

1. Tape one numeral in the center of a different plate.

2. Line the plates up from 1 to 5.

3. Count out the correct number of pennies for each plate and put them on the plates.

4. Then put all the pennies back in the cup.

5. Now mix up the plates. Can you put the correct number of pennies on each plate?

Going Further

1. Encourage the children to have some fun with the pennies. Can you build a house with them? a sunshine with rays? What other things can the children build? You and the other children should try guessing the identity of children's various penny constructions.

2. Build a pile of the pennies. Can the children get all the pennies in one pile?

3. Have the children count out five pennies each. Then ask them to pitch the pennies into a plastic container or bowl. After each child has pitched his or her pennies, ask the child to count how many pennies went into the bowl and how many landed on the floor.

4. Have the children examine the pennies with a magnifying glass, looking at the numerals, letters, and pictures.

5. In ten coin tosses, how many heads and how many tails did each child get?

Activity III-A3. Pasta Wheels

Materials Needed

- copy of "Pasta Wheels" worksheet
- nine pasta wheels
- markers or crayons
- glue

Directions for Children

1. Color the pictures with your markers or crayons.
2. Count the number of wheels on the wagon.
3. Count out that number of pasta wheels.
4. Glue the wheels in the circles under the wagon.
5. Then do the same with the other pictures.
6. Count all the wheels on your worksheet.
7. How many pictures have one wheel? How many have two wheels?

Going Further

Let the children help you cook some pasta wheels. Add a little sauce, margarine or oil. Serve a few pasta wheels to each child on a small plate. Can they count their pasta wheels before they eat them?

Pasta Wheels

Activity III-A4. Bird's Nest

Materials Needed

- copy of "Bird's Nest" worksheet
- crayons or markers
- glue
- scissors

Note to Teacher

You can vary the number of eggs the children are to glue onto the worksheet by whiting out the numeral and printing another numeral (from 1 to 5) before making copies of the worksheet.

Directions for Children

1. Color the bird's eggs.
2. Color the bird.
3. Color the nest.
4. Cut the strip of eggs off the top of the worksheet.
5. Cut on the solid lines to separate the eggs. Your teacher can help you with this.
6. Look at the number under the nest. Count out this number of eggs and glue them onto the nest.

Going Further

Try to find an empty (old) bird's nest in the neighborhood around the school and bring it to class. Let the children examine the empty nest and talk about what it's made of. Then, each day, put a different number of paper or plastic eggs in the nest for the children to count.

3

Activity III-A5. Turkey Feathers

Materials Needed

- copy of "Turkey Feathers" worksheet
- brown, green, red, and yellow felt
- oaktag or cardboard
- glue

Note to Teacher

Using the worksheet as a pattern, cut a turkey out of brown felt and glue it to the piece of cardboard. Cut out fifteen feathers from the other felt. Then cut apart the number cards and place them face down on the table.

Directions for Children

1. Pick a number card. Count the dots and say the number.
2. Count out that many feathers and put them on the turkey.

Going Further

Put a bowl of shelled peanuts or popcorn, along with the number cards (from the "Turkey Feathers" worksheet) laid face down, on a table. Have two children take turns picking a number card, saying the number, and counting out that many pieces of snack.

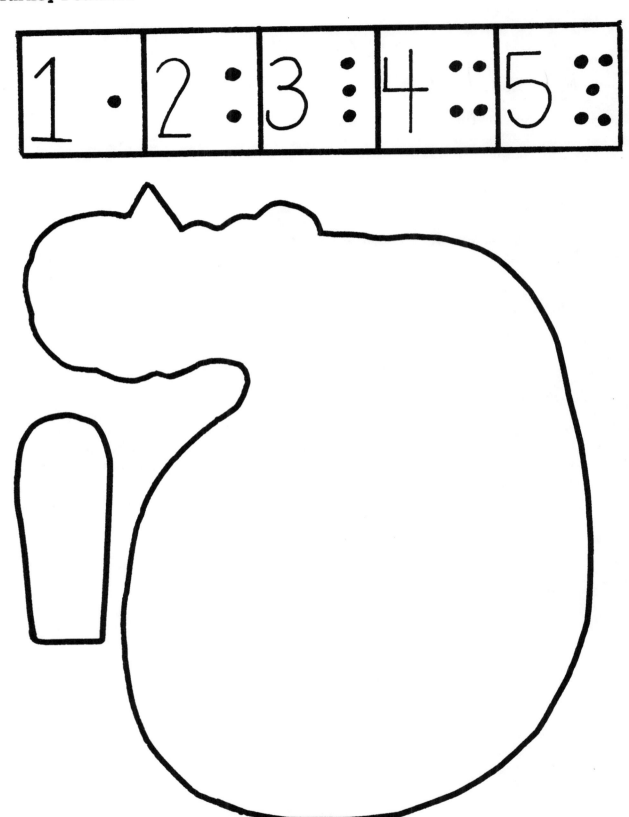

Activity III-A6. Roll and Count

Materials Needed

- copy of "Roll-and-Count Cube" worksheet
- tape
- oaktag
- small plate of popcorn

Note to Teacher

Glue the worksheet onto oaktag and cut along the solid lines. Fold the flaps into the center square so that the numerals and dots are on the outside of the cube. Tape all the edges in place.

Directions for Children

1. Roll the cube. What number is on the top of the cube? You may take this number of pieces of popcorn from the plate.
2. Continue until the plate is emptied.
3. When there isn't enough popcorn on the plate for your number on the cube, you have to keep rolling the cube until you get that number.

Going Further

Fill a bowl with small wooden beads (the kind used for threading are good). Let the children take turns with an egg carton and the roll-and-count cube. Each child rolls the cube and takes the number of beads shown on top of the cube. The child then places one bead in each compartment of the egg carton.

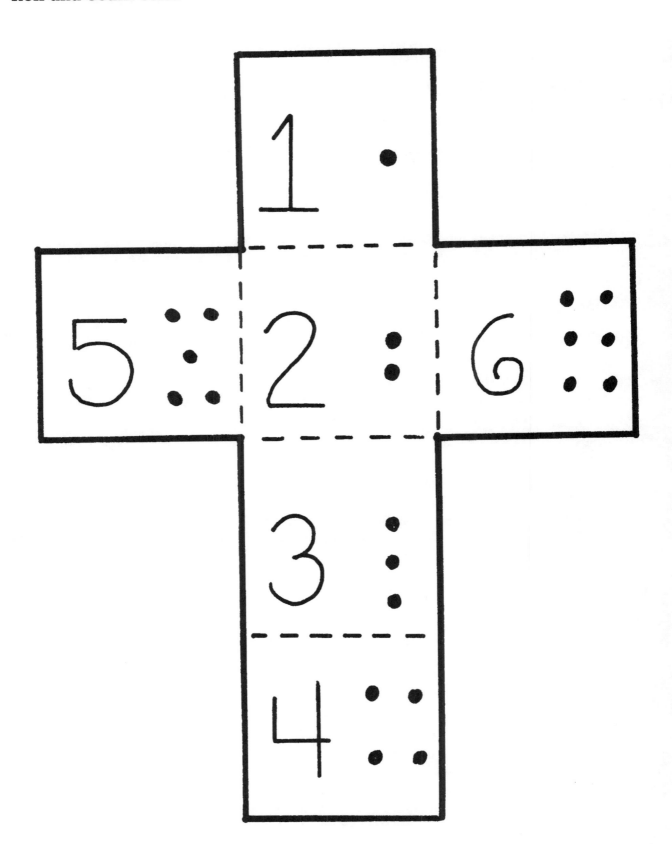

Activity III-A7. Squirrel's Delight

Materials Needed

- white construction paper
- crayons or markers
- scissors

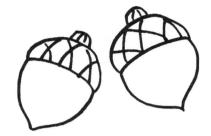

Note to Teacher

Go on an outdoors "hunt" with the children to look for oak trees and acorns. Bring along a bag so that the children can pick up some fallen acorns and examine them back in the classroom. When on the oak tree/acorn hunt outside, be sure to look for and watch squirrels, too. You might want to display pictures of squirrels, oak trees, and acorns in the room.

Directions for Children

1. Draw and color five acorns on your paper.
2. On another sheet of paper, draw and color your own oak tree with a squirrel nearby.
3. Cut apart the five acorns from the paper.
4. How many acorns does the squirrel want to hide in the tree? Your teacher will tell you how many acorns.
5. Put that number of acorns on your oak tree.

Going Further

Gather a collection of real acorns and hide them around the classroom. Say, "Let's be squirrels" and have the children pretend to be squirrels hunting for dinner. The children can count the number of acorns they have found.

III-B. RECOGNIZING NUMERALS

Purpose

The recognition of numerals gives the children a 'name' to give to a group of objects. After counting a given set of objects, the children will be able to 'name' the group with a recognized numeral. The development of this visual discrimination skill is basic to the math process.

Activity III-B1. Number Puzzles

Materials Needed

- copy of "Number Puzzles" worksheet
- glue
- thin cardboard
- markers
- four self-locking plastic bags
- scissors
- newspaper to cover work area

Directions for Children

1. Look at each numeral on the worksheet. Draw and color in that number of apples in each box.
2. Then spread glue evenly on the cardboard and lay your worksheet on the cardboard. Let it dry.
3. Your teacher will help you cut apart the four number puzzles.
4. Your teacher will then help you cut each puzzle into three or four pieces.
5. Put each puzzle in its own plastic bag.
6. Choose a bag and do the puzzle. Count the apples on each puzzle and look at the numeral that is next to it.
7. Do the other puzzles in the same way.

Going Further

Have a "Preschool Apple Day" with the following activities:

1. Draw a big apple on each of five pieces of construction paper, and write one numeral (1, 2, 3, 4, 5) in the center of each apple. Have on hand a bag of 15 small

apples. Line up the apple papers in order from 1 to 5. Have the children take turns putting the correct number of apples on each paper. If the children are proficient in recognizing numerals, mix up the numerals and have them count out the apples again.

2. Make apple sauce with the children, allowing them to cut up (with a plastic knife) the apples you have peeled and cored. Discuss the parts of the apple as you prepare the apples.

Apple Sauce Recipe

Cut apples into chunks. (Count the chunks.) Add a little water and cook in a saucepan or slow cooker until apples are soft. Mash the apples. Add cinnamon (and honey) to taste. Spoon the apple sauce into small cups and enjoy!

3. Give each child an apple core (saved from making the apple sauce). Help them to break apart the core and pick out the seeds. Can the children count their seeds?

4. Cut an apple in half across its middle and ask the children if they can see anything (a "star") in the middle of the apple. Pour a thin layer of tempera paint into a shallow styrofoam or aluminum pan. Dip the apple half into the paint. On a piece of construction paper, have each child print the apple several times. Count the number of prints and write that numeral on the paper.

Try this again but with an apple cut sideways. Let the children compare the two prints.

5. Teach this poem to the children:

Way Up in an Apple Tree

Way up in an apple tree
Two little apples smiled at me. (*hold fists up in the air*)
I shook the tree as hard as I could. (*make motion as if shaking a tree*)
Down came the apples (*flitter fingers from up to down*)
And m-m-m-m were they good! (*rub tummy*)

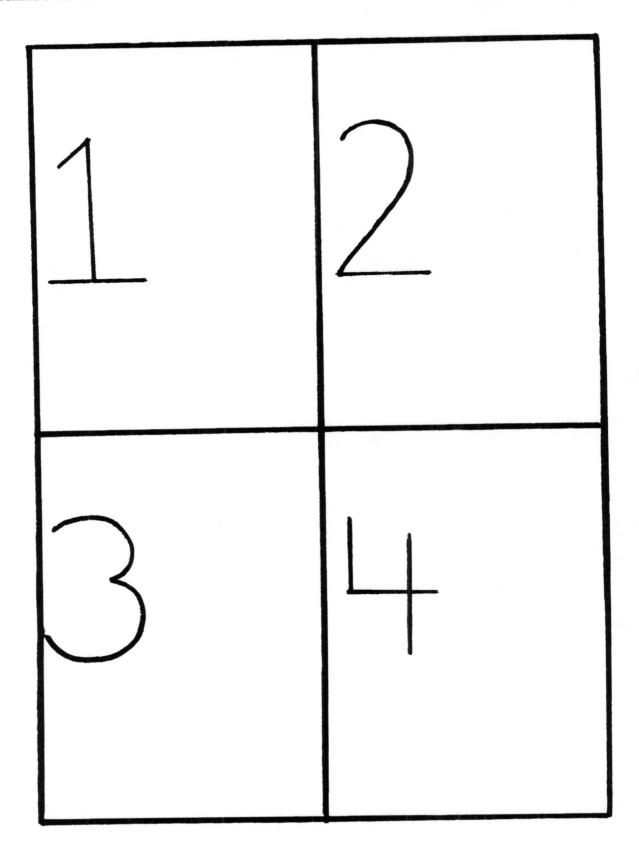

Activity III-B2. Apple Picking

Materials Needed

- child's drawing of a recognizable tree
- brown, green, and red felt
- set of teacher-made numeral/dot cards (from 1 to 4)
- oaktag or cardboard
- two small plastic bags
- scissors
- glue

Note to Teacher

Use a child's drawing of a recognizable tree as a pattern to cut a tree top out of green felt, a tree trunk out of brown felt, and ten apples out of red felt. Glue the tree to the oaktag or cardboard, and put the ten apples in a small plastic bag.

Make a set of 2″ × 2″ cards showing the numerals 1, 2, 3, 4 with their corresponding number of dots. Put the cards in the other small plastic bag.

Directions for Children

1. Close your eyes and take a card out of the plastic bag.
2. Count the number of dots next to the numeral.
3. Take that number of apples out of the other plastic bag and put them on the tree.
4. Continue in the same way for the other cards.
5. When all the apples are on the tree, put the numerals back in the bag.
6. Now take a numeral out of the bag. Take that many apples off the tree.
7. Continue until there are no more apples on the tree.

Going Further

You can do the same activity with different cut-outs, such as a black felt rectangle and white stars for a nighttime scene. Ask your children for ideas and help the children to make them. The children will enjoy seeing their suggestions materialize!

Activity III-B3. "Seedy" Cards

Materials Needed

- fifteen dried (pepper or melon) seeds
- five index cards
- glue
- markers

Directions for Children

1. Write one numeral from 1 to 5 on a different card.
2. Glue one seed on the other side of the "1" card, two seeds on the "2" card, three seeds on the "3" card, four seeds on the "4" card, and five seeds on the "5" card.
3. Let the cards dry.
4. Pick up one card and count the number of seeds. Turn the card over and look at the numeral.
5. Do this with the other "seedy" cards.

Going Further

1. Ask the children to put the cards in order from 1 to 5 with the seed side up. Now have the children mix them up and put them in order with the number side up. Increase the number of seed cards to ten.

2. For each child, put a flower seed on one side of a sheet of paper. Let each child draw a picture of one flower on another sheet of paper. Continue on up to five. Then have the children match the number of seeds to the number of pictured flowers.

Activity III-B4. Feeling Numbers

Materials Needed

- sand
- five index cards
- glue
- newspaper to cover work area

Directions for Children

1. With the glue, write the numeral 1 on one of the index cards.
2. Sprinkle sand on the card. Shake off the excess and let it dry.
3. Do the same for the numerals 2, 3, 4, 5.
4. When all the cards are dry, turn them over and put the appropriate number of drops of glue on the cards. Sprinkle the drops with sand, shake off the excess sand, and let the drops dry.
5. Now, close your eyes and pick up one card. Move your finger over the sand number. Turn the card over and move your finger over the sand dot(s), saying the number of dots you feel.
6. Do this with all the other cards.

Going Further

Draw one sand bucket on each of the five index cards. Cover the bucket lightly with glue; then sprinkle sand to make five different levels of sand in the buckets. Let the cards dry. Then mix up the cards and have the children line up the buckets from least to most sand.

Activity III-B5. Pepper Seeds

Materials Needed

- green (or red) pepper
- copy of "Pepper Seeds" worksheet
- markers
- scissors
- glue

Note to Teacher

Cut the pepper in half so the children can see the many seeds one pepper produces. Show the children different colored peppers (green, red, yellow—and even black).

Directions for Children

1. Cut apart the four peppers along the solid lines.
2. Color the peppers.

3. Look at the numeral under each pepper. Draw that number of dots inside each pepper.

4. Then put a drop of glue on each dot.

5. Lay a seed on each drop of glue.

Going Further

Cut a pepper in quarters the long way and give a quarter to each group of four children. Have the children pick out the seeds and wash the pepper quarter. Help the children cut up the pepper quarters with a plastic knife and stick a toothpick in each piece to enjoy as a snack.

You might also have the children compare the flavors of green, red, and yellow peppers.

Activity III-B6. Surprise Pizza

Materials Needed

- copy of "Surprise Pizza" worksheet
- crayons
- scissors
- glue

Directions for Children

1. With a crayon, color the five pizza toppings at the bottom of the worksheet. Color the pizza crust.

2. On the pizza, draw five circles.

3. In each circle, draw the number of dots to match each numeral on a topping.

4. Cut the strip of toppings from the bottom of the worksheet. Then cut each topping apart along the black lines.

5. Now, count the dots on one of the circles on the pizza.

6. Find the numeral topping for that number and glue it onto the pizza.

7. Continue until you have all your numeral toppings on your pizza.

8. What could these toppings be?

Going Further

Your class can make pizza dough knots. Have the children wash their hands. Then give each child a piece of pizza dough (ready-made in the refrigerated case of the dairy department or in the frozen food section of the supermarket). Have the children flatten their dough out on a floured surface. With a plastic knife, they can cut the dough into strips. Help the children to knot the strips and place them on a greased cookie sheet; brush with oil and bake at 400°F. until brown (about 15 minutes). Which knot is the largest? the smallest? the longest? the shortest?

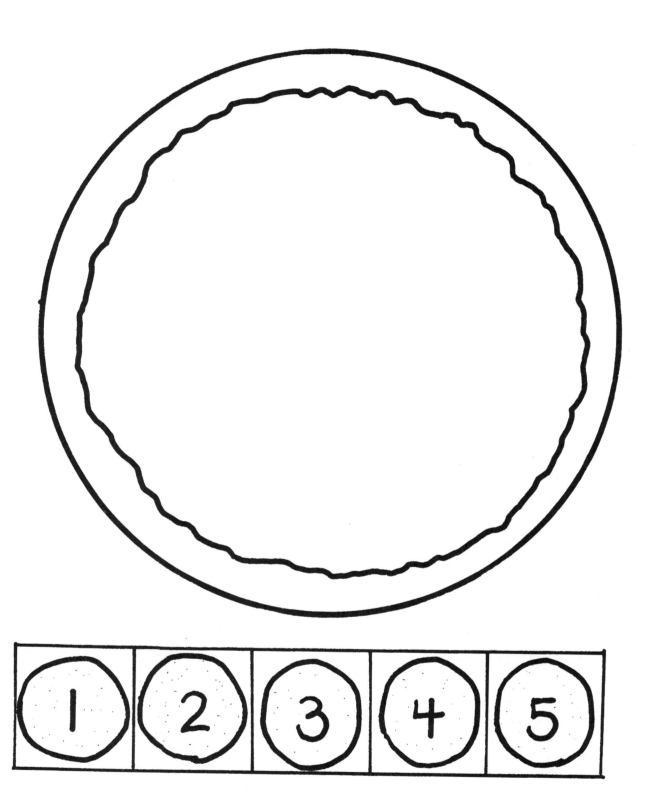

III-C. ONE-TO-ONE CORRESPONDENCE

Purpose

One-to-one correspondence activities help children develop the concept that things can be matched by their quantity and their qualities. The children will be developing their visual discrimination skills, as well as their concrete counting skills. This development will aid in promoting their pre-reading and pre-math readiness.

Activity III-C1. Corresponding Objects

Materials Needed

- copy of "Corresponding Objects" worksheet
- at least six of each of the following objects placed in a shoe box
    —paper clips
    —buttons
    —empty thread spools
    —1-inch oaktag squares
    —1-inch oaktag triangles
    —pennies

Directions for Children

1. Look at the top left box on your worksheet.
2. What is the item? How many are there?
3. Find that many objects in the shoe box.
4. Count as you place each object over its picture.
5. Continue until you fill the worksheet.

Going Further

Using five index cards, draw one peanut shape on the first card, two on the second, and so on. From a bowl or bag of peanuts, have the children place a real peanut on top of each drawn peanut. Ask the children to count the peanuts on each card as they are put back in the bowl.

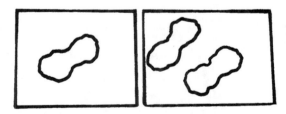

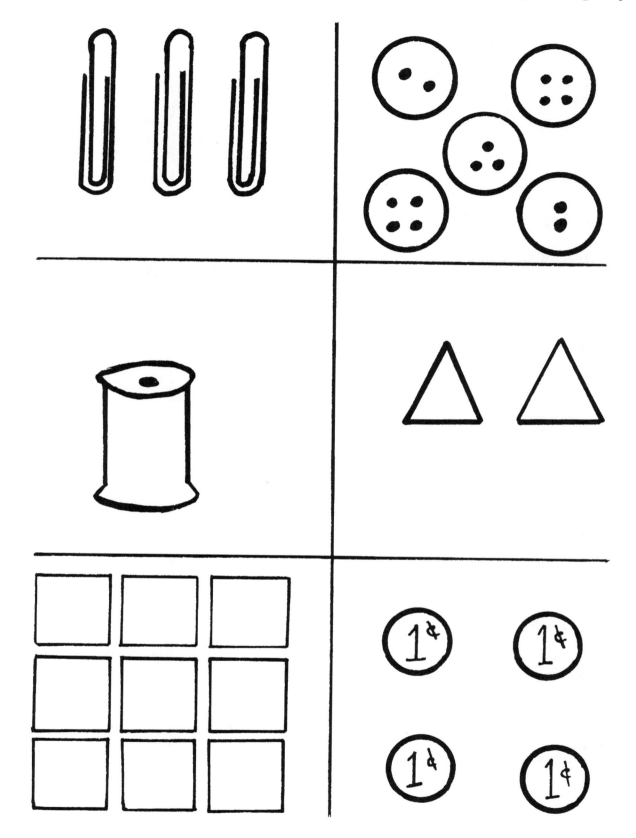

III-D. MORE/LESS

Purpose

The concept of 'more or less' is a basic math skill that sets the foundation for the higher level skill of estimation. Through these hands-on activities, the children will be counting, observing and beginning to understand that quantities have relationships to one another.

Activity III-D1. The Marble Mystery Box

Materials Needed

- shoe box divided and cut as shown
- ten marbles
- two small plastic plates
- two rubber bands

tape cardboard divider to box

hand hole   *? ? ? ?*   *hand hole*

Note to Teacher

Put a different number of marbles in each side of the box. Put the top on the box and secure it with the rubber bands.

Directions for Children

1. Put your hand in one of the hand holes in the box. Feel the marbles.
2. Take one marble at a time and count it while putting it on the plastic plate.
3. Again, count the marbles on the plate.
4. Now do the same with the other side of the box and the other plate.
5. Can you tell which plate has more marbles? How did you figure that out?

Going Further

1. Instead of marbles, use hard-shelled nuts such as walnuts, pecans, or almonds.

2. You'll need fifteen acorns and five small plastic deli-salad containers with lids (washed and dried). Write one numeral from 1 through 5 on a different lid. Put one acorn in a container, two acorns in another container, and so on. Have the children count the number of acorns in any one container, then choose the corresponding lid to put on the container.

III-E. SORTING/MATCHING

Purpose

Sorting and matching are important preschool skills for children to master. Engaging in a variety of these activities will help the children develop visual discrimination skills. These skills will aid in their ability to see the difference between a 'p' and a 'q', between an 'n' and an 'm', and so on. This fine tuning of their observation skills is essential in these pre-reading years.

Activity III-E1. Button Matching

Materials Needed

- copy of "Button Matching" worksheet
- collection of four-of-the-same buttons in a small box

Directions for Children

1. Look at how the two buttons on the top of your worksheet match.
2. Pick a button out of your box and put it in a square below one of the matching buttons on the worksheet.
3. Now pick out another button. Does it match the button you put on the worksheet? If it does, put it next to the button. If it doesn't, put it in another square below the button.
4. Continue until you have matched all the buttons.

Going Further

Gather a collection of 24 two-of-the-same buttons. Have the children sort them into the twelve cups in an egg carton.

Activity III-E1
Button Matching

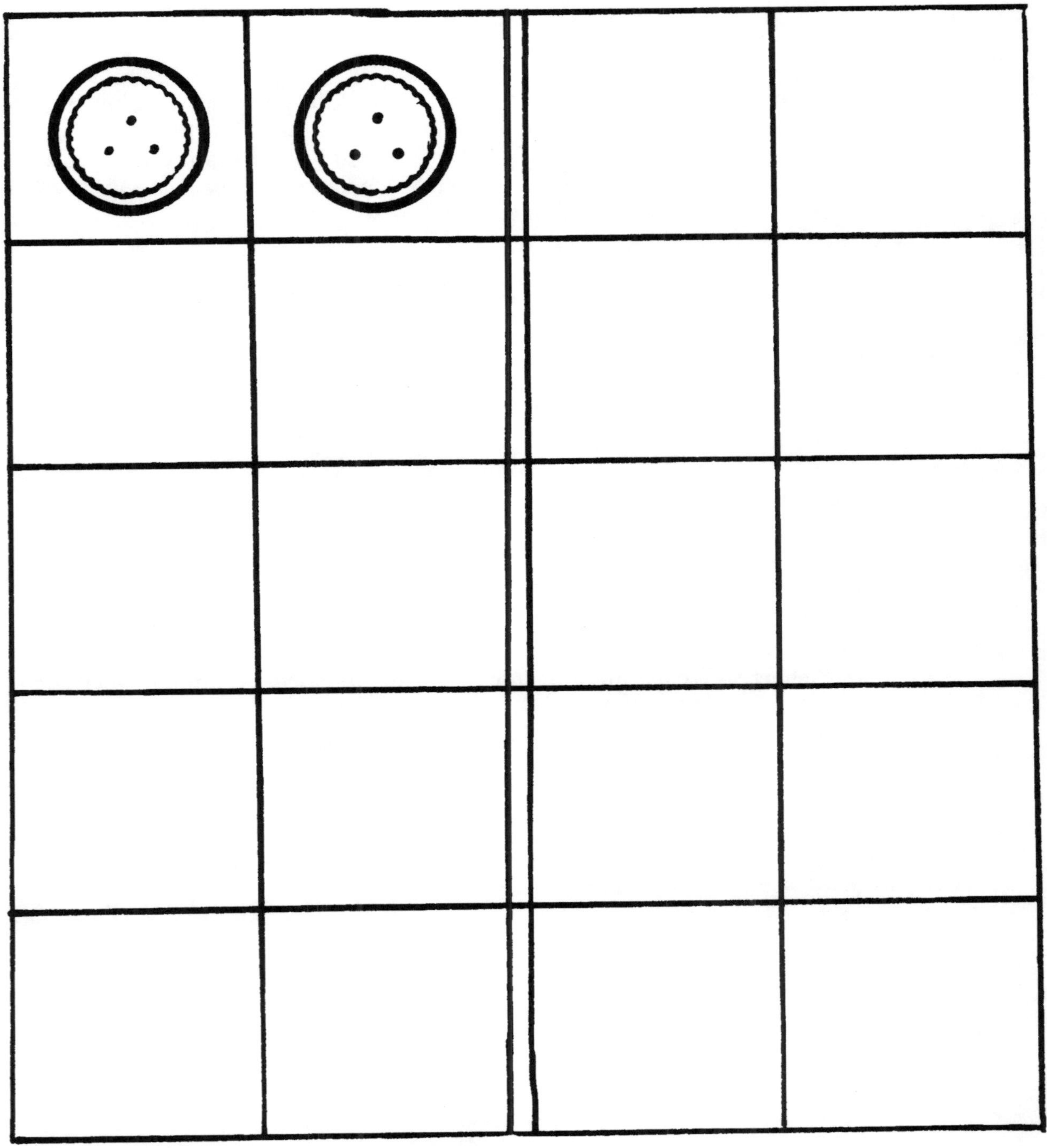

Activity III-E2. Balancing

Materials Needed

- pan balance scale
- twenty pennies

Directions for Children

1. Count out three pennies and put them in one of the pans.
2. Now, one at a time, add pennies to the other side and watch the pans move. How many pennies did you have to put in to make the balancing arm straight?
3. Continue to experiment with different numbers of pennies. What do you notice when there is the same amount in each pan? When you take out one penny? When you add three pennies?

Going Further

Have available small rocks, blocks, and wooden beads with which to experiment. Ask the children, "How many wooden beads do you need to balance one block?" Have the children think of other balancing experiments.

Activity III-E3. Seashell Hunt

Materials Needed

- shoe box with about three inches of sand in it
- variety of small shells

Note to Teacher

Hide the shells in the sand.

Directions for Children

1. Dig with your hand for the shells in the sand.
2. Group them according to size, color, shape, or in some other way.
3. When you've found all the shells, count each pile. Which pile has the most? the least?

Going Further

Make clam shell boats. With a permanent marker, write one of the numerals (1 through 5) on the inside of five different clam shells. Have the children use chips to count out the correct number of "passengers" for each boat.

Activity III-E4. Equal Sets

Materials Needed

- copy of "Equal Sets" worksheet
- oaktag or cardboard
- markers or crayons
- glue
- scissors

Directions for Children

1. Color the marbles in each matching set the same color.
2. Glue the worksheet onto the oaktag.
3. Your teacher will help you cut apart the sets. Make two piles of the cards.
4. Now, mix up the cards in each pile.
5. Pick one card and put it on the table in front of you. Count the marbles on the card.
6. Look through the other set of cards to find the one that matches this one.
7. Put it next to its match.
8. Continue until all the set cards match.

Going Further

With a marker, divide five index cards in half. Draw a large circle on both sides of each card. In the circle on the left-hand side of one of the cards, trace around one penny; on the left-hand side of the next card, trace around two pennies; and so on. Give a child a bowl of at least fifteen pennies. The child must lay in the right-hand side circle of each card the number of pennies needed to make the two sets equal.

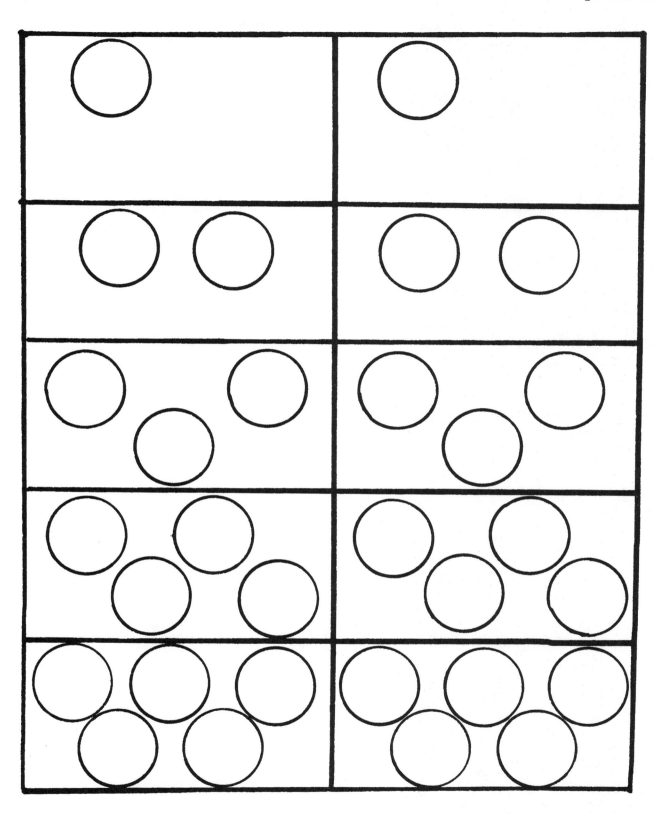

IV. Shapes and Letters Discovery Center

The activities in this center are designed to focus the children's attention on detail awareness. If children can tell the difference between a square and a rectangle, or a circle and an oval, then they are ready to move on to recognizing the difference between an E and an F, and so on. The Shapes and Letters Discovery Center begins with hands-on shape activities so that the children can see, feel and play with shapes, and then moves into letter recognition activities.

Shapes and Letters Discovery Center Management Sheet

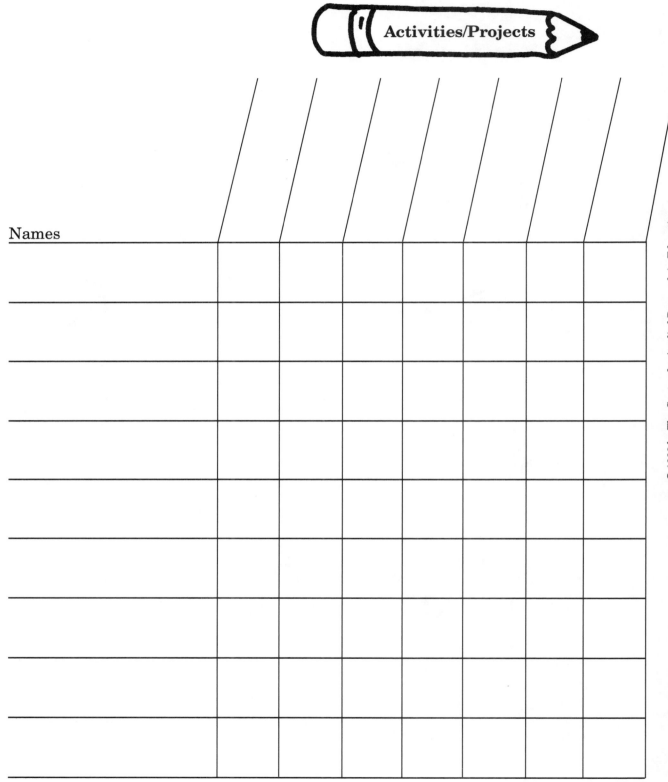

Activities/Projects

Names

Shapes and Letters Discovery Center Management Sheet

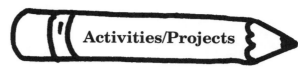

Activities/Projects

Names

IV-A. SHAPES

Purpose

In order for children to master the identification of alphabet letters, they must become aware of the differences between the letters and conscious of the details that define each letter. To begin your children along the path to alphabet recognition mastery, you must help them first develop a good command of shape recognition.

Getting Started

Shapes are all around us. Show a round dinner plate and ask, "What else do we have that is round?" What other shapes can the children find in the classroom? (rectangular windows, oval eggs, square floor tiles, triangular sandwich halves, rectangular doors)

When the children are sitting for snack, walk around the room and say, for example, "I see an orange square. Can you guess what it is?"

Activity IV-A1. Sorting Shapes

Materials Needed

- five small plastic plates
- assortment of construction paper triangles, squares, rectangles, ovals, and circles in a small box

Note to Teacher

Tape one of each shape to the center of a different plate.

Directions for Children

1. Take one shape out of the box. Look at it carefully.
2. Match it to one of the shapes on the plates. Put it on that plate.
3. Continue until you have matched all the shapes in the box.

Going Further

Make a shape traffic light. Discuss the reasons why we have traffic lights, and what each color on the traffic light means. Show pictures of traffic lights or walk around the neighborhood with the children to look at the various traffic lights. Then give each child a copy of the "Traffic Light" worksheet. Have the children color the two shapes and identify them. On another sheet of paper, have the children draw, color, and cut out a red circle, a yellow circle, and a green circle. Ask the children to pick the circle that means "stop" and glue it at the top part of the rectangle on the worksheet. Below that circle, the children then glue the circle that means "be careful" (caution). At the bottom, the children glue the circle that means "go."

Activity IV-A2. Floating Shapes

Materials Needed

- sponges cut into one of each shape: square, triangle, circle, oval, rectangle
- dishpan half full of water

Directions for Children

1. Float your shape sponges in the water.
2. Close your eyes and feel for a sponge.
3. When you have found one, feel it all around and try to guess what shape it is.
4. Open your eyes. Were you right?
5. If you were right, squeeze all the water out of the sponge and put it on the table. If you were not right, put it back and try again!

Going Further

Pour a thin layer of tempera paint into a styrofoam or tin pan. Have the children dip one of the shape sponges in the paint and print it on a piece of construction paper. Continue with the other sponge shapes.

Activity IV-A3. Sugar Cube Towers

Materials Needed

- small bowl of sugar cubes (or wooden cubes)
- glue

Directions for Children

1. Put one cube on top of another.
2. See how many you can pile up before they fall over.
3. What might you be able to build using sugar cubes and glue? Try it!

Going Further

Print A, B, C (and other letters) on paper and make copies for the children. They can then place sugar cubes over the letter patterns.

Activity IV-A4. Circle Chain

Materials Needed

- seven 2-inch construction paper circles with a small pencil-point hole punched through
- seven 1½-inch pieces of drinking straws
- 15-inch length of yarn with a large knot on the end
- plastic blunt needle (OR wrap a piece of cellophane tape around the start of the yarn OR dip the start of the yarn in white glue and let it dry OR put clear nail polish on the start of the yarn and let it dry)
- markers or crayons

Directions for Children

1. Decorate your circles with stripes or dots.
2. String a piece of the straw on your yarn.
3. Then string on a circle.
4. Repeat the circles and straws until you have used all the straw pieces and all the circles.
5. When finished with the chain, tie the ends of the yarn together. Your teacher can help you with this. How can you use your circle chain?

Going Further

Have the children make a square chain, a rectangle chain, or a triangle chain in the same manner as the circle chain. Or, ask the children to think of how to make a shape chain using various shapes.

Activity IV-A5. A Triangle Pineapple

Materials Needed

- copy of "A Triangle Pineapple" worksheet
- pile of small light-brown triangles
- glue
- markers or crayons

Directions for Children

1. Color the top of the pineapple.
2. Color the bottom of the pineapple.
3. Glue the triangles upside down ∇ all over the pineapple.

Going Further

Bring in a real pineapple for the children to feel, smell, and observe. Peel and slice it for a special treat. Have plenty of napkins available for this juicy snack!

Activity IV-A6. Hanukkah Stars

Materials Needed

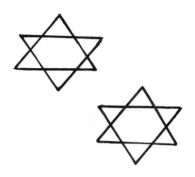

- drawing paper
- crayons or markers
- scissors
- glue
- light-blue construction paper
- glitter

Note to Teacher

Check your local library for some children's books that tell the story of Hanukkah and share these stories with the children.

Directions for Children

1. Draw six triangles. Color two triangles with one crayon. Color another two triangles with another crayon. Color the last two triangles with a third crayon.
2. Cut out the triangles.
3. Glue them onto your construction paper to make stars for Hanukkah.
4. Then decorate your paper with glue and glitter.

Going Further

Make Hanukkah cards. Have the children fold a sheet of construction paper in half and decorate the front of the card with stars made from small triangles. Help the children to write a Hanukkah greeting inside the card.

Activity IV-A7. Fishing for Shapes

Materials Needed

- copy of "Fishing for Shapes" worksheet
- nine paper clips
- cellophane tape
- old magazines and/or store advertisements
- scissors
- fishing pole made from a dowel, yarn, and magnet

Note to Teacher

Cut out the shapes on the worksheet. Cut out three magazine pictures of toys and glue them on the squares. Cut out three pictures of animals and glue them on the circles. Cut out three pictures of fruits and glue them on the triangles. Tape a paper clip to the other side of each shape. Lay all the shapes, picture-side down, on the floor.

Directions for Children

1. Let's fish for shapes.
2. What shape have you caught with your fishing pole? What kind of picture is on the shape?
3. Make three separate piles of fruits, toys, and animals you have caught.

Going Further

Tie a strong magnet to the end of a fishing pole. Tape a heavy-duty paper clip to plastic attribute shapes. (If you don't have attribute shapes, use construction paper shapes.) Lay the shapes on the floor. Have the children fish for shapes and classify them according to shape, color, or size.

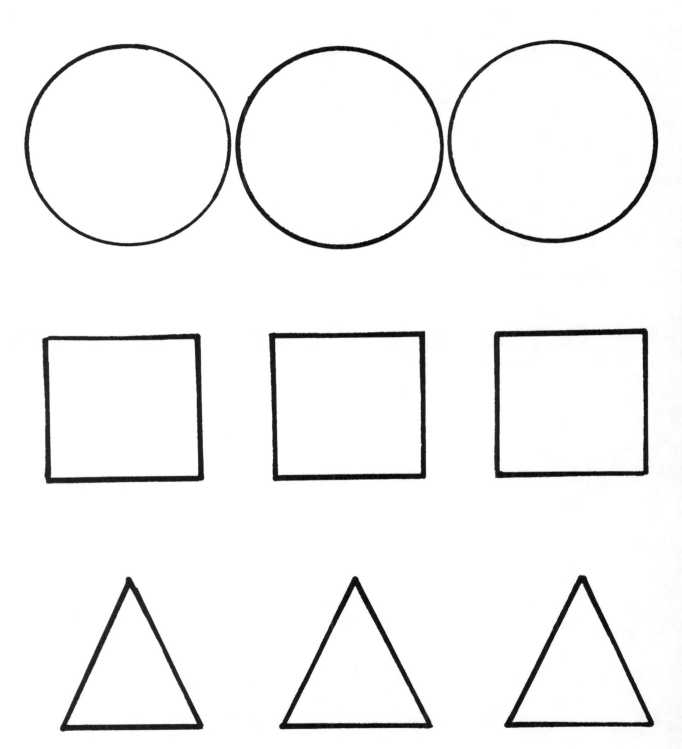

Activity IV-A8. Muffin Tin Sorting

Materials Needed

- copy of "Muffin Tin Sorting" worksheet
- two sheets of construction paper
- scissors
- six-cup muffin tin
- small box

Note to Teacher

Using the worksheet as a pattern, place it on top of the two sheets of construction paper and cut out all the shapes. Put the shapes in the small box.

Directions for Children

1. Look at the shapes.
2. Sort the six different shapes into the six muffin cups.

Going Further

Use the muffin tin to sort round and square threading beads by color, size, and shape.

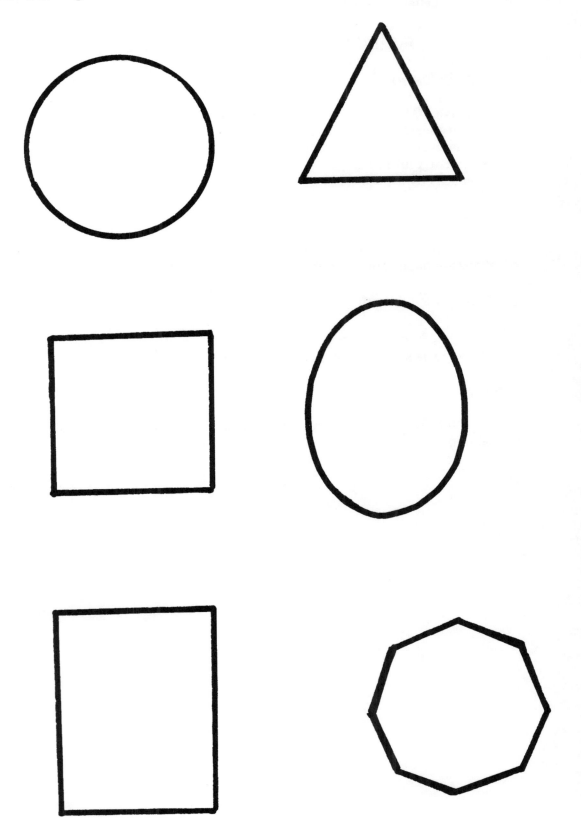

Activity IV-A9. A Shape Feel Box

Materials Needed

- attribute blocks (three triangles and three circles)
- shoe box with one hole cut into each end for hand holes
- rubber band

Note to Teacher

Open the shoe box and put three triangles and three circles inside. Put the lid on the box and secure it with a rubber band.

Directions for Children

1. Put your two hands into the hand holes and feel the shapes.
2. Try to find a triangle. When you think you have found one, take it out of the box. Are you right?
3. Continue feeling for triangles.
4. Make a pile of triangles. Then make a pile of circles.

Going Further

1. Put similar shapes into the box, such as rectangles and squares; triangles and octagons.

2. Put large and small balls in the box to be felt and classified.

3. Put hard and soft, or smooth and rough objects in the box to be felt and classified.

IV-B. LETTERS

Purpose

The visual recognition of alphabet letters, coordinated with the concept that thing have 'names' made up of letters, is a basic pre-reading skill. Before you can read a word you must be able to recognize letters. Through these activities children will become 'comfortable' with letters.

Activity IV-B1. Letter Boxes

Materials Needed

- five boxes with lids
- assortment of pictures and plastic items that start with the letters A, B, C, D, E; for example:

A	B	C
apple	banana	comb
apron	balloon	cotton
acorn	bell	candle
airplane	bandage	car
arrow	ball	crayon
ace playing card	bee	carrot

D	E
duck	elephant
donut	eraser
dog	egg
dinosaur	elastic
deer	eagle
doll	

Directions for Children

1. Read the letter on one of the boxes.
2. Take the top off the box.
3. Take each item, one at a time, out of the box and name it.
4. When you are finished, put the items back, one at a time, while saying what it is again.
5. Do the same with the other letter boxes.

Going Further

Can the children think of other items that can be put into each particular box?

Activity IV-B2. Label Your Classroom

Materials Needed

- copy of "Label Your Classroom" worksheet
- drawing paper
- markers or crayons
- scissors
- masking tape

Directions for Children

1. Color the pictures on your worksheet. What other things might you find in your classroom? Draw and color some of these on a sheet of paper.
2. Cut out the worksheet pictures on the solid black lines. Cut out your own pictures, too.
3. Take one of the pictures and find that object in your classroom.
4. Tape the picture to the object.
5. Continue with the other pictures.

Going Further

Make labels for the things in your play area, such as the sandbox, a tree, a swing, a bush, a gate, and so on.

Window

Door

Table

Easel

Chair

Plant

Activity IV-B3. Pretzel Letters

Materials Needed

- copy of "Pretzel Letters" worksheet
- box of stick pretzels

Note to Teacher

This activity deals with straight-line letters of A, E, F, H.

Directions for Children

1. With your finger, go over all the letters on the worksheet. The letters are all made from straight lines.
2. Take the stick pretzels and place them on the worksheet to form Pretzel Letters.
3. Now you can eat each of your letters!

Going Further

Have the children try making these letters on plain paper without the patterns. Ask, "What other letters can you make with these pretzels?"

Activity IV-B3
Pretzel Letters

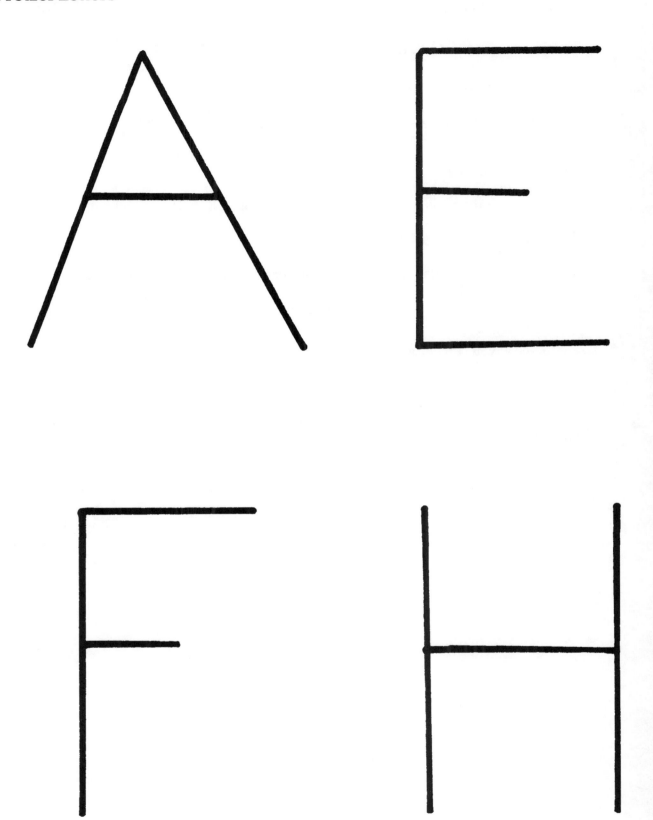

Activity IV-B4. Clay Letters

Materials Needed

- copy of "Clay Letters" worksheet
- clay

Note to Teacher

This activity deals with curved letters of B, C, D, and G.

Directions for Children

1. Roll your clay into "snakes."
2. Use your clay snakes and form them on the worksheet to make clay letters.

Going Further

1. Have the children try making these letters on plain paper without the patterns. Ask, "What other curvy letters can be made with the clay?"

2. Instead of clay, have the children help you make salt dough (recipe below). The children can then form letters with the salt dough and let the letters harden. The letters can be painted.

Salt Dough Recipe

Mix together 4 cups flour, 1 cup salt, 1½ cups water, and 1 tablespoon cooking oil. Knead this dough for about 5 minutes.

3. The children can write the letters of their names in clay or salt dough.

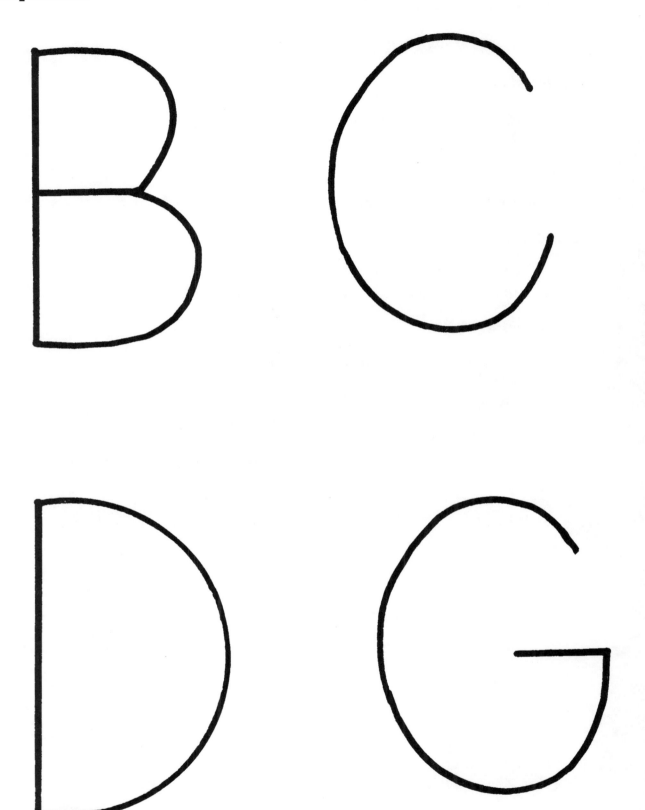

Activity IV-B5. A, B, C, D

Materials Needed

- drawing paper
- markers or crayons
- teacher-made A, B, C, D cards
- glue

Note to Teacher

Make a set of four cards for each child. Each card should have one of the letters (A, B, C, D) printed on it.

Directions for Children

1. Draw and color pictures of an apple, ball, carrot, and door.
2. Say the name of each picture.
3. Pick out the letter that starts each word and glue it onto the picture.

Going Further

Help the children find these real items (apple, ball, carrot, door) in the classroom. Can they find anything else that starts with these letters? Do any of the children's names start with A, B, C, or D?

Activity IV-B6. My Initial Plaque

Materials Needed

- salt dough (see Activity IV-B4 for the recipe)
- pencil
- bag of dried green split peas

Directions for Children

1. Roll the dough into a ball about the size of an orange.
2. Press the ball into a pancake about ¼-inch thick.
3. With light pressure, make your first name's initial in the clay with a pencil.
4. Press the dried peas into the dough.

5. Let the dough air dry or your teacher can bake the plaque in a 325° oven for 30 minutes.

Going Further

1. You might want to spray the children's plaques with mat Verathane shellac or varnish.

2. The children can make a hole in the top of the plaque with a pencil before the plaque hardens. After it hardens, the children can string their plaques with yarn and hang them up.

V. Five Senses Discovery Center

Our five senses help us discover, appreciate, and communicate with the world in which we live—they are natural teaching machines. We hear, taste, touch, smell, and see thousands of stimuli each day. Hearing a dog bark, autumn leaves rustle, or a faucet drip are all sounds that conjure up mental pictures in our mind. The smell of an apple pie baking brings an emotional response quite different from the smell of a house on fire. Our tongues communicate the wonderful world of flavors and textures, determining our likes and dislikes. The softness of a kitten and the roughness of sandpaper are messages sent to our brains through our fingers. Sight allows us to savor with our eyes nature's beauty. Children use their senses so automatically that they usually don't appreciate them. In this Center, the children will become actively aware of what their eyes, ears, nose, tongue, and fingers do!

149

Five Senses Discovery Center
Management Sheet

Activities/Projects

Names

Five Senses Discovery Center
Management Sheet

Activities/Projects

Names

V-A. SIGHT

Purpose

Our sense of sight is our most used sense. The moment we open our eyes after birth, we begin our learning. Although a baby's vision is fuzzy for the first two months of life, these blurry images make their impact on the child. Sharpening young children's observation powers will greatly aid them in their ability to distinguish the details and subtle differences in every-day objects and, later on, in letters and words when they begin as young readers. Focusing on familiar objects around them will help the children note the difference between the letters q and p or between the words car and care.

This section will help hone your children's observation and pre-reading skills, and prepare them to be "discoverers" of the world around them.

Getting Started

Opportunities for diverse experiences when using our sense of sight are endless. When you are walking the children to the playground, ask them to name the colors of the leaves on the trees, the color of the bark, the color of the sky. Which of these does *not* change color? Can they see any clouds, any other children, any animals or birds?

In the classroom, ask the children if they see "something living" (plants, classroom pets) or "something that moves" (clock's second hand, mobile in a breeze, fish in a tank).

Teach this little song to the children:

"My Five Senses"

I have eyes that can see (*point to eyes*)
and a nose that can smell. (*point to nose*)
I have fingers that can touch (*wiggle fingers*)
and they do it very well.
I have ears that can hear (*point to ears*)
and a tongue that can taste. (*stick out tongue*)
These five things I should never waste.

Note to Teacher

The skill reinforced by each "Sight" activity is included.

Activity V-A1. Sorting Seeds by Color and Shape

Skill: visual discrimination

Materials Needed

- copy of "Seed Wheel" worksheet
- markers or crayons
- small box (with a lid) containing an assortment of seeds including: apple seeds, orange seeds, watermelon seeds, and pea seeds
- magnifying glass

Note to Teacher

Display a variety of these foods and their seeds for the children to examine.

Directions for Children

1. Color all seeds and foods on the Seed Wheel.

2. Pick out a seed from the box and look at it carefully with the magnifying glass. Do this with other seeds from the box, too.

3. Now look at the Seed Wheel again. Does any seed on the wheel match any of the seeds from the box? If it does, put the seed in the section of the wheel that it matches. If it doesn't match any of the seeds on the wheel, put it in the box's lid.

4. Do the same with the rest of the seeds in the box.

Going Further

1. Gather a collection of dried seeds of assorted shapes, sizes, and colors. Have the children glue them on a piece of construction paper to make a "Seed Collage." (Remind the children that they only need one tiny drop of glue for each seed.)

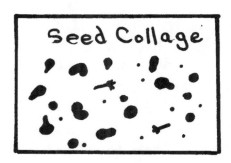

2. Reinforce one-to-one correspondence with the children. Help the children press a variety of fall leaves. Then photocopy several different kinds of leaves—one leaf per sheet of paper. Make a pile of photocopies and a pile of leaves. Then ask the children to match the leaves with the photocopies.

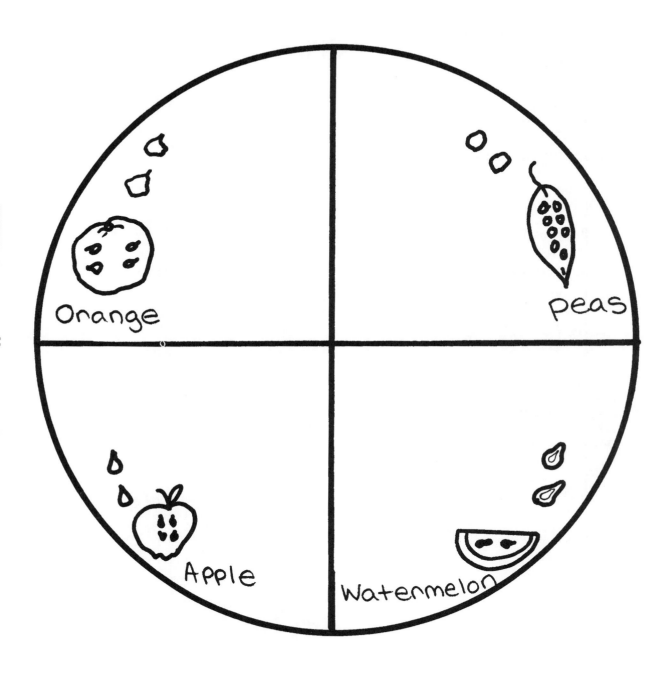

Orange

Peas

Apple

Watermelon

Activity V-A2. What's Missing?

Skill: visual detail awareness

Materials Needed

- copy of "What's Missing?" worksheet
- markers or crayons

Directions for Children

1. Look carefully at the top left picture on your worksheet.
2. Now look at the picture next to it on the right. What's missing?
3. If you think the leaves of the flower are missing, you are correct. Draw two leaves on the flower.
4. Now look at the other pictures and figure out what is missing from each.
5. When you are finished, color all the pictures.

Going Further

Make a "What Goes Together?" game. Collect two of each kind of item; for example, two Lego® pieces, two small blocks, two buttons, two plastic straws, and so on. Put one of each item in a shoe box and the other of the same item in another shoe box. Have the children pick one item out of one of the boxes and put it on the table in front of them. They then look for that same item in the other shoe box. When they find it, they put it next to its match. The children continue until they have matched all the items.

Activity V-A3. Carrots

Skill: visual discrimination

Materials Needed

- copy of "Carrots" worksheet
- orange crayon
- scissors
- glue
- white construction paper with a line drawn down the middle

Directions for Children

1. Look at the carrots on your worksheet. A rabbit has nibbled at some of them. Point to the ones that have been nibbled.

2. Color all the carrots.

3. Cut out all the carrots on the black line around each carrot. Your teacher will help you with this.

4. Make a pile of the nibbled carrots and a pile of the whole carrots.

5. Glue the nibbled carrots on one side of the construction paper and the whole carrots on the other side of the paper.

Going Further

Bring in a bag of real carrots. Open the bag and let the children look at the different sizes and shapes of the carrots. Have the children line them up from shortest to longest.

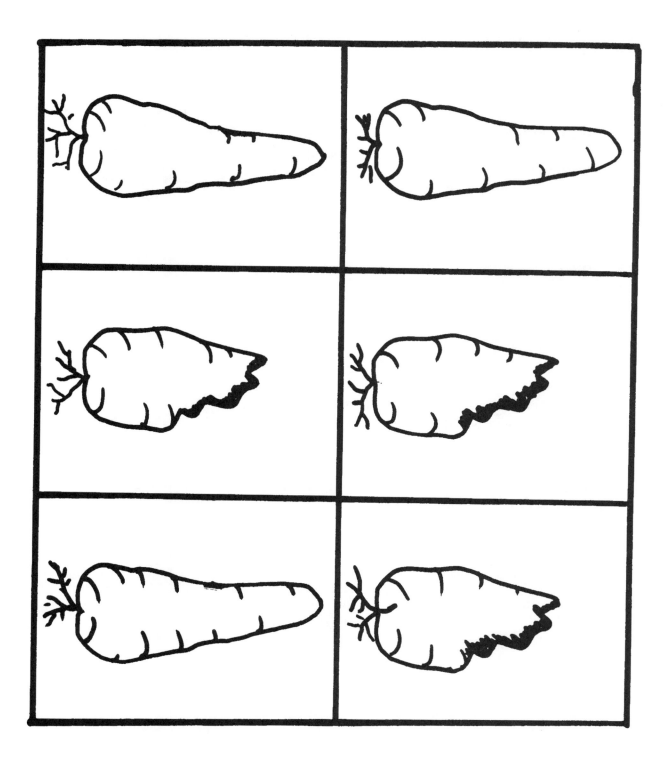

Activity V-A4. All in a Row

Skill: visual discrimination

Materials Needed

- copy of "All in a Row" worksheet
- self-locking plastic bag
- scissors
- different light colors of felt
- flannel board

Note to Teacher

Use the worksheet as a pattern to cut out five of each flower from light-colored felt.

Line up one of each kind of flower on the left-hand side of the flannel board, and mix up the rest of the flowers and put them in a pile for the children.

Store the felt flowers in the plastic bag when not in use.

Directions for Children

1. Pick one flower from the pile. Look at it carefully.
2. Look at the three flowers on the flannel board. Which one does your flower match?
3. Put your flower next to the one it matches.
4. Continue with the rest of the flowers until you have three rows of all the same flowers.

Going Further

With the children, look around your school grounds for any flowering bushes, such as forsythias, rhododendrons, and lilacs. Look carefully at their flowers and leaves. Ask the children to look to see if they find any of these bushes in their neighborhood when they go home. Do the same for flowers or flowering trees.

Activity V-A5. Subtle Differences

Skill: visual detail awareness

Materials Needed

- four identical color paint sample strips (most paint stores are happy to donate these strips from discontinued paint colors)
- construction paper
- scissors
- glue
- self-locking plastic bag

Note to Teacher

Cut three of the paint strips into individual shades and put them into the plastic bag.

Cut the shades from the remaining strip. Glue them in a sequence from dark to light, down the left-hand side of the construction paper.

Directions for Children

1. Take a color sample from the bag and match it to one of the shades on the construction paper.
2. Lay the color sample next to the shade it matches.
3. Do the same with the other shades in the bag.

Going Further

1. Ask, "What color are the walls in the classroom?" "Are any of the walls in your house or apartment that color?" "Are there any toys in the classroom that are the same color as the walls?" "Is anyone in the classroom wearing anything that is the same color as the walls?"

2. Cut a six-inch circle out of oaktag and tape colored cellophane over the opening. The children can take turns seeing their world in different colors.

3. Play "What's Missing?" Set out a variety of common objects, such as a pencil, a small ball, a block, and a button. Cover the objects with a cloth. Then "sneak" your hand under the cloth and select one object. Lift it up along with the cloth. Ask, "What's missing?" Increase the number of objects set out as the children get more proficient at the game.

Activity V-A6. A Tisket, a Tasket, a Yellow Fruit Basket

Skill: color discrimination

Materials Needed

- red, orange, green, and yellow felt
- copy of "Fruit Basket Patterns" worksheet
- scissors
- flannel board
- tape player
- blank tape
- headphone

Note to Teacher

Use the fruit basket patterns to cut out a basket from yellow felt, an apple from red felt, an orange from orange felt, a pear from green felt, and a banana from yellow felt.

Record on the tape player this song to the tune of "A Tisket, A Tasket":

A tisket, a tasket, put up my yellow basket, my basket, my basket.
Now my yellow fruit basket needs some fruit, some fruit, some fruit.

Can you find an apple, an apple, an apple?
If you can find an apple, put it in my basket, my basket, my basket.

A tisket, a tasket, now my yellow basket needs an orange, an orange, an orange.
Can you find an orange, an orange, an orange?
If you can find an orange, put it in my basket, my basket, my basket.

A tisket, a tasket, now my yellow basket needs a pear, a pear, a pear.
Can you find a pear, a pear, a pear?
If you can find a pear, put it in my basket, my basket, my basket.

A tisket, a tasket, now my yellow basket needs a banana, a banana, a banana.
Can you find a banana, a banana, a banana?
If you can find a banana, put it in my basket, my basket, my basket.

Now look at my basket, my basket, my basket.
Now look at my basket, it's full!

Take away the apple, the apple, the apple.
Take away the apple, out of my basket.

Take away the orange, the orange, the orange.
Take away the orange, out of my basket.

Take away the pear, the pear, the pear.
Take away the pear, out of my basket.

Take away the banana, the banana, the banana.
Take away the banana, out of my basket.

Directions for Children

Listen to the tape and follow the directions using the fruit and the flannel board.

Going Further

Put together a real fruit basket. Bring in a wicker basket and ask each child to bring in a piece of fruit to put in the basket. Discuss the size, shape, and color of the fruit as the basket is filled. Then have a fruit-tasting party.

Activity V-A7. Observing Shapes

Skill: visual shape discrimination

Materials Needed

- copy of "Observing Shapes" worksheets (two pages)
- glue
- oaktag
- markers or crayons

Note to Teacher

Glue the worksheet showing the separate shapes onto a piece of oaktag. Then color the shapes as indicated and cut out the shapes.

Directions for Children

1. Look at the shape picture worksheet.
2. Match the oaktag shapes to the proper places on the shape picture.
3. Take the shapes off the worksheet.
4. Then color the shapes on your worksheet using the same colors as the oaktag shapes.

Going Further

Have the children look around the classroom for objects that have the same shape as the oaktag shapes; for example, a triangle block, a square box, a round plate, an oval plastic egg, a rectangle book.

Orange

red

yellow

brown

Activity V-A8. Recycling Bottles, Cans, Newspapers

Skill: visual item discrimination

Materials Needed

- copy of "Recycling" worksheet
- crayons or markers
- scissors
- glue

Directions for Children

1. Color the bottles, cans, and newspapers at the bottom of the worksheet.

2. Then cut out all the recyclables. Your teacher will help you with this.

3. These recyclables must go into their proper containers. Look carefully at each item and its container at the top of the worksheet to make sure you are putting the item in the proper place.

4. Glue the recyclables on top of the appropriate recycling container on the worksheet.

Going Further

1. Discuss with the children why we recycle. Bring in and display a variety of recyclables; then have the children sort the items. Ask your local recycling plant if tours for school children are available or if someone from the plant could visit the classroom.

2. Play "I Spy." Start by saying "I spy..." and the children say, "What do you spy?" You might then say, for example, "I spy something brown and soft." (Give the children a chance to look around the room and guess.) If they haven't guessed, add more clues, such as "It has two shiny button eyes"...and so on.

     You might also read *Each Peach Pear Plum*, an "I Spy" story by Janet and Allan Ahlberg.

3. Put pictures of four recyclable objects on the flannel board and name the objects with the children. Ask the children to close their eyes while you remove one object. Ask, "What's missing from the flannel board?" When the item is named, put it back on the flannel board and repeat the procedure. Add more objects to increase the game's challenge.

4. Put photos of four of the children in your class on a bulletin board. Say the names of the children in the photos. Then have all the children close their eyes while you remove one photo. Ask, "Whose picture is missing?" Continue to play as described. Change and/or add more photos.

V-B. HEARING

Purpose

Children will develop an awareness of the many sounds and words we use to help us communicate. Through these simple games and activities, the children will sharpen their listening and direction-following skills.

Tuning into sounds is also an invaluable step toward developing the skill to hear phonetic variations when the children begin to learn to decode words.

Getting Started

Ask the children to close their eyes and listen carefully to any classroom sounds they might hear (wind rustling the curtains or blinds, street sounds, children in other classrooms, and so on).

Continue by asking the children if they can recognize some sounds that you will make, such as closing your desk drawer, ringing a bell, slamming a book closed, blowing a whistle.

On the playground, have the children sit in a circle and listen for outdoor sounds (children playing, dogs barking, car or truck horns blowing, airplanes flying overhead, and so on).

Activity V-B1. Shake Cans

Materials Needed

- copy of "Shake Cans" worksheet
- three 35mm film containers
- pennies
- sand
- marbles

Note to Teacher

Fill each container with one of the above sound makers. Make sure the top of the container is snapped on securely.

Directions for Children

1. Shake each container and try to guess what is in the container.

2. Look at the pictures on the worksheet and place each container on the picture it matches.

Going Further

1. After the children have mastered these three sounds, try some more: water, paper clips, rice, buttons, flour.

First, elicit from the children possible reasons that objects make different sounds. Explain that objects that shake back and forth very fast send out something that we call "sound waves." (To demonstrate this to the children, look at a tank of water and how the water can be made to have waves.)

Echoes are sound waves that hit hard objects and bounce back. This can happen in a cave, a hallway, and other places. Experiment by having the children shout "hello" into a small bucket. Even if they don't hear an actual echo, they will hear an interesting distortion of the sound waves.

2. Have a variety of large sea shells available for the children to listen to. The shells' smooth, hard chambers echo and re-echo surrounding noises, which blend to produce the wonderful sound of the sea.

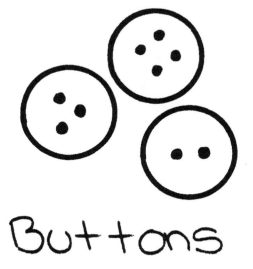

Buttons

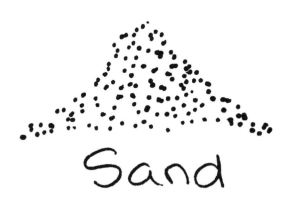

Sand

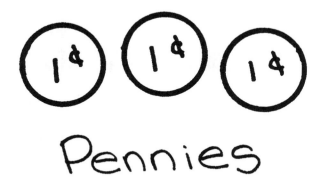

Pennies

Activity V-B2. Instrument Listening Game

Materials Needed

- bell
- triangle
- drum
- rhythm sticks
- maraca
- two children

Note to Teacher

Demonstrate and name the instruments to be used in this game. Then ask two children to sit with their backs to each other. One child has all the instruments. The other child is the "guesser."

Directions for Children

1. The child with the instruments, choose one instrument and make a sound.
2. The "guesser," try to guess which instrument was just played.
3. Continue the game with the other instruments.
4. Now switch positions and continue the game.

Going Further

1. Let the children help you fill several glasses with different amounts of water. Then have the children carefully tap each glass with a metal spoon and listen to the different sounds each glass makes. Can they try to play a song with these water-filled glasses?

2. With crayons or markers, have the children decorate the bottoms of two small white paper plates and both sides of a tongue depressor or craft stick. Have the children put a spoonful of dried beans on one of the plates; then help them invert the other plate and staple the two plates together. Before completely stapling the plates together, insert the craft stick between the edges of the plates and staple it in place as the handle. The children can now shake and listen to the beans hitting against each other and the plate in these handmade maracas.

Activity V-B3. Copy-Cats

Materials Needed

- two bells
- two wooden sticks
- two pieces of paper
- two tin cans and two pencils
- two hard-covered books
- two children

Note to Teacher

Ask two children to sit on chairs with their backs to each other. In front of each child is a table containing a set of the above sound makers.

Directions for Children

Children, take turns making a sound with one of your sound makers; the other child, you must make the same sound with your sound makers.

Going Further

1. Have a tape recorder available at your next parent/teacher (or similar) meeting. Ask each parent to record a short message to his or her child. (Keep a list of the order in which you record the parents.) Play a portion of the tape to the children at several Morning Circles, instructing the children to listen carefully for a message from someone they know.

2. Likewise, you can record the children's voices for the parents to identify. It's great fun to play these tapes along with slides of the children "in action" for an Open House presentation. The children can explain what they are doing in the particular slide.

Activity V-B4. Guess the Story

Materials Needed

- tape recorder with microphone
- three blank tapes
- headphone
- three favorite story books

Note to Teacher

Record onto the blank tapes three of the children's favorite stories. Use props or your voice to make the story "come alive."

At the end of each story, ask, "Do you know the name of this story?" (pause)

Then ask one or two simple listening questions about events in the story; for example, "What was the sound that the mother duck made?" (pause) "What did the wolf say when he wanted to blow down the pig's house?" (pause)

Directions for Children

1. Put on the headphone and play the tape.

2. Listen carefully.

Activity V-B5. Listen! Attribute Shape Game

Materials Needed

- set of attribute shapes in a box
- tape recorder
- blank tape
- headphone

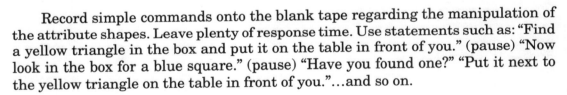

Note to Teacher

Record simple commands onto the blank tape regarding the manipulation of the attribute shapes. Leave plenty of response time. Use statements such as: "Find a yellow triangle in the box and put it on the table in front of you." (pause) "Now look in the box for a blue square." (pause) "Have you found one?" "Put it next to the yellow triangle on the table in front of you."…and so on.

Directions for Children

1. Put on the headphone and play the tape.

2. Listen carefully.

Activity V-B6. Listen to What Simon Says

Materials Needed

- tape recorder
- blank tape
- headphone

Note to Teacher

Record on the blank tape simple "Simon Says" commands, such as: "Simon says clap your hands twice." (pause) "Simon says put one finger in the air." (pause) "Simon says hold your nose." (pause)...and so on.

Directions for Children

1. Put on the headphone and play the tape.
2. Listen carefully.

Going Further

Read *Noisy Books* by Margaret W. Brown to the children. Encourage the children to listen for the sounds around their neighborhood.

Activity V-B7. Musical Finger Painting

Materials Needed

- finger paints
- finger-painting paper
- tape recorder
- teacher-made tapes or commercially available tapes
- headphone

Note to Teacher

Record a variety of music in different tempos. Two cassettes/records that are great for this finger-painting activity are: *Happy Hour* (Melody House)—a happy upbeat fully-instrumental recording, and *Quiet Time* (Melody House)—soothing traditional and classical music.

Directions for Children

1. Put a dollop of finger paint on the finger-painting paper.
2. Move your finger paint around the paper while listening to the music.

3. Have the children show their finger paintings to one another. How are they similar or different from one another?

Activity V-B8. Animal Sounds

Materials Needed

- tape recorder
- blank tape
- headphone
- teacher-made animal cards

Note to Teacher

1. Photocopy pictures of common animals or cut them out of old magazines. Glue the pictures onto a large sheet of oaktag.

2. On the blank tape, record the sounds of the animals you've put on the oaktag. The children can all participate in making the cassette. Or, you can tape the appropriate animal sounds from commercially-prepared cassettes/records, such as: *Walk Like the Animals* (Melody House) and *Animal Antics* (Melody House). IMPORTANT: Recreating sounds is a skill that is developed after a lot of practice in listening and tuning in to sounds. If a child is unable to recreate simple sounds, incorporate more listening exercises into your day.

3. Give instructions at the beginning of the tape telling the listener to point to the picture of each animal that is heard on the tape. You could also include some details about each animal's characteristics or habitat.

4. You might also include instructions and a pause for the listener to make the animal sound: "Now you make the animal sound that you just heard." (pause)

Directions for Children

1. Put on the headphone and play the tape.

2. Listen carefully.

Activity V-B9. Listen and Make a Colorful Design

Materials Needed

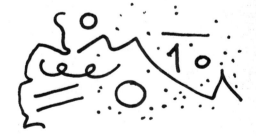

- tape recorder
- blank tape
- headphone
- eight-color box of crayons
- drawing paper

Note to Teacher

Record instructions on the tape, such as: "Now we are going to make a colorful design using all eight colors of crayons you have. Have your drawing paper ready and your crayon box opened. Pick out your green crayon. Make green dots all over your paper. (pause) Now put your green crayon back and take out your blue crayon. Make some blue lines on your paper. (pause) Now put your blue crayon back and take out your yellow crayon. Make some circles or O's with your yellow crayon." (pause)...and so on.

Directions for Children

1. Put on the headphone and play the tape.
2. Listen carefully.

Going Further

It would be fun for the children to see an exhibit of these drawings and to note how—even with the same colors and directions—the final designs are all different!

Activity V-B10. Listening Walk

Materials Needed

- tape recorder (optional)

Note to Teacher

Take the children on a listening walk around the neighborhood or through the school building. To help the children focus their attention on sounds, ask a few open-ended questions, such as, "What kind of sounds do you think we will hear if we take a walk around the block?" "To make sure we hear all the sounds, what should we do?" "If we walk inside our school building, what kind of sounds do you think we might hear?"

As you walk, encourage the children to tell you the sounds they hear using such descriptive words as "loud laughter," "hard banging," "soft brushing."

If you take along a tape recorder, you can review and enjoy the sounds again back in the classroom.

Going Further

Ask the children to listen to the sounds in each of their rooms at home. Discuss some of the possible sounds they might hear in the different rooms:

Kitchen
electric can opener
refrigerator door opening
  and closing
pot of water boiling
water running

Bedroom
clock ticking/alarm ringing
radio playing
drawers opening and closing

Bathroom
shower running
someone brushing his/her teeth
toilet flushing

Living Room
television playing
people talking
vacuum cleaner

You might send home a ditto for each child and an adult or sibling to work on together to write the sounds heard.

Activity V-B11. Listen and Match

Materials Needed

- twelve empty plastic eggs
- egg carton
- small amount of each of the following:
    —rice
    —flour
    —pennies
    —small paper clips
    —marbles

Note to Teacher

Fill two plastic eggs each with the items mentioned in the materials list and tape the eggs closed.

Directions for Children

1. Shake one egg and listen carefully to its sound. Put it in the egg carton.

2. Now shake the other eggs until you find the one that sounds like the first one you picked.

3. When you find it, put it next to the egg in the egg carton.

4. Continue until you have "sound-matched" all the eggs.

Going Further

1. Sing "Old MacDonald's Farm" with the children. After singing the song with the whole class making all the animal sounds together, divide the class into different animal groups. Then sing the song again, this time having three or four sheep going "baa, baa," cows going "moo, moo," horses going "neigh, neigh," and pigs going "oink, oink."

2. Play a recording (or make one with the children) of jungle animal sounds, such as a gorilla growling, a lion roaring, an elephant bellowing, and a tropical bird squawking. Repeat the sounds more than once if you are making the recording; or, play the tape over and over again until the children can differentiate among the animal sounds.

3. Have each child bring in something from home that makes a noise; for example, a wind-up clock, a battery-operated toy dog that barks or a toy car that honks, a doll that cries, an egg beater, a portable radio, a music box. Let the children take turns making their sound for the other children whose eyes are closed. You might bring your class—with the sound makers in hand—to another classroom in your school to try this sound game on those children.

V-C. TOUCH

Purpose

The children will discover that their hands and their sense of touch are very special. We begin by emphasizing the uniqueness of each child's handprint. Then, the children will be moving through activities that make them aware of all the many ways we use our hands to accomplish self-help activities, such as getting dressed, eating, drinking, and washing ourselves. By touching things that are hard and soft or rough and smooth, the children will grow to appreciate their marvelous sense of touch.

Getting Started

Ask the children such open-ended questions as, "What are some of the first things you do when you get up in the morning?" "How do you use your hands to do those things?" "When you come to school, what do you use your hands for?" "Feel this piece of sandpaper. Now feel this piece of oaktag. Tell me how they feel." "Let's all clap with our hands." "Let's shake each other's hand and say, 'Welcome.'"

Activity V-C1. My Special Hands

Materials Needed

- any color tempera paint in a small bowl
- small chubby paintbrush
- piece of construction paper taped to newspaper
- pail of water, sponge, and paper towels

Directions for Children

1. Carefully brush tempera paint onto your palm and fingers.
2. Press your painted hand down on the construction paper.
3. Paint and press your hands until you've filled your construction paper with your hand prints.
4. Clean up by washing your hands in the pail of water.

Going Further

Sing these songs with the children:

—"Open, Shut Them"
—"Hands and Fingers, Knees and Toes"
—"Peter Piper"

These songs can be found on *Joy: Songs for Early Childhood* (Sadlier, Inc., New York).

Activity V-C2. A Rainbow of Hands

Materials Needed

- large piece of kraft paper taped to the floor, with three rainbow bands drawn on it
- tempera paints in small bowls
- one small chubby paintbrush for each paint color
- pail of water, sponge, and paper towels

Directions for Children

1. Paint your hand with a color.
2. Print your hand in one band of the rainbow.
3. Repeat until you've covered the whole first section with hand prints of one color. Your prints can overlap.
4. Wash and dry your hand.
5. Paint your hand with another color.
6. Print your hand in the next band of the rainbow.
7. Continue until you have filled this whole section with hand prints of a second color.
8. Wash and dry your hand.
9. Now do the same with a third color in the last section of your rainbow.
10. Hang your "Rainbow of Hands" on the wall.

Going Further

Have each child print his or her hand on a legal-sized envelope. Write "Things (child's name) Likes to Touch" on the envelope. Let the children cut out pictures from old magazines or store/supermarket flyers of things they like to touch and put these pictures in their envelopes. Review a few of the envelopes from time to time with the whole class.

Activity V-C3. Hand Puppet

Materials Needed

- copy of "Hand Puppet" worksheet
- brown lunch bag
- crayons or markers
- glue

Directions for Children

1. Color the two pieces of your hand puppet.

2. Cut them out. Your teacher will help you with this.

3. Glue the head of your puppet on the bottom flap of your bag. Glue the body of your puppet to the long side of the bag under the flap.

4. Put your hand in the bag and close your fingers into the flap of the bag.

5. Open and close your hand to make your puppet open and close its mouth.

Going Further

1. Encourage the children to use their hand puppets for making up stories and/or conversations.

2. Using an overhead projector and a screen, have the children use their hands to make shadow puppets. (Their hands should be placed near the glass plate on the overhead projector.) Can the children think of ways to make a bunny and other animals?

Activity V-C4. Things I Like to Touch

Materials Needed

- copy of "Things I Like to Touch" worksheet
- markers or crayons

Directions for Children

1. Look at your worksheet. Make believe the hand in the middle is your hand.
2. Look for something on the page that you would like to touch.
3. Draw a line from the hand to that object.
4. Continue until you have drawn lines from the hand to all the things you would like to touch.
5. Now, color the hand and all those things you would like to touch.

Going Further

1. Gather actual materials for the children to feel and decide if they like to touch them or not.

2. Send home a small brown lunch bag with a note to the parents to put a small object that belongs to their child in the bag and staple or tape it closed, and return it with their child to school. At "Touching Something That's Mine" time, distribute the bags and have the children close their eyes, feel what's in their bag, and guess before taking it out of the bag.

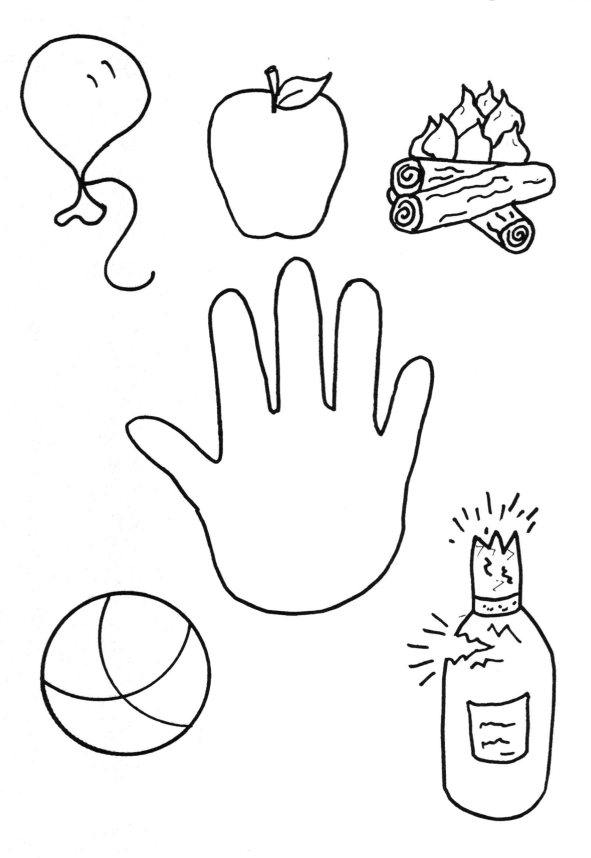

Activity V-C5. My Fingers Can Feel

Materials Needed

- copy of "My Fingers Can Feel" worksheet
- shoe box with a hand hole cut in one end
- rubber band
- real objects to correspond with the pictures on the worksheet
- crayons or markers

Note to Teacher

Put all of the real objects in the shoe box and close it with a rubber band.

Directions for Children

1. Color the pictures on your worksheet.
2. Now look at one of the pictures on your worksheet.
3. Put your hand in the hole in the shoe box. Can you find that object?
4. When you have found the object, put it on top of its picture on your worksheet.
5. Try to do the same thing with all the other objects in the box.

Going Further

1. Show the children how to place their fingers on their throats. Then have them softly say "Boooooooo." Can they feel the vibration the word makes as it comes up their larynx? Experiment with other words and phrases.

2. Glue (or tape) onto oaktag a crayon, a button, a small block, a paper clip, an unsharpened small pencil, or any other small available objects. Then put a matching object in each of five brown lunch bags. Ask the children to close their eyes and reach inside each bag and determine what the object is before taking it out of the bag. The object is then to be placed next to the matching object on the oaktag.

Crayon

Marble

Button

Rubberband

Cottonball

Small Block

Activity V-C6. Soft Collage

Materials Needed

- cotton balls
- feathers
- scraps of foam, yarn, flannel, and carpeting
- construction paper
- glue

Directions for Children

1. Pick up one of the materials. Feel how soft it is.
2. Put a drop of glue on your construction paper and put your soft material on the glue.
3. Continue with all your other pieces of soft things.

Going Further

Play "Simon Says." Since children this age do not have refined listening skills, play this simple version.

Teacher: "Do what Simon says. Simon says touch the table."

Children all touch the table.

Teacher: "Is the table hard or soft?"
Children: "Hard."
Teacher: "Simon says touch your cheek."

Children touch their cheeks.

Teacher: "Is your cheek hard or soft?"...and so on.

Use other things such as floor, hair, chair, hand, and book.

V-D. SMELL

Purpose

Our sense of smell is used for both enjoyment (cookies baking) and protection (smoke and fire). Children will focus on the pleasures we get from smelling flowers, fruit, chocolate, and so on.

Getting Started

What could smell better than fresh popcorn popping? Having the children watch—and smell—as you pop some popcorn is a great way to peak their interest in this section. Discuss how our sense of smell sparks our appetite to taste and eat a variety of foods. Also, elicit from the children suggestions of things that may smell good to some children but not to others. Our sense of smell is very particular to each one of us; it's another uniqueness that makes us all different and special.

Activity V-D1. The Smelling Game

Materials Needed

- copy of "The Smelling Game" worksheet
- four empty margarine tubs with small holes punched in the lids, in which small amounts of the following are placed:
  —soap
  —popped popcorn
  —chocolate chip cookie
  —apple slice

Directions for Children

1. Look at the worksheet and name each of the objects on it.
2. Choose a tub.
3. Look again at your worksheet. Which of those objects does this tub smell like?
4. Put the tub on top of that picture.
5. Do the same with the other tubs.
6. When you have finished, peek under each lid to check if you are correct.

Going Further

Set out small bowls of different flavors of popcorn, such as cheese-flavored, butter-flavored, plain, and barbecue-flavored. Have the children close their eyes and try to identify the different varieties by using their sense of smell.

Activity V-D2. Make and Smell Ice Cream Cones

Materials Needed

- copy of "Ice Cream Cones" worksheet
- crayons or markers
- cotton balls
- different kinds of fruit extracts
- glue

Directions for Children

1. Color the two cones on your worksheet.

2. Spread glue on the top part of one of the ice cream cones.

3. Lay the cotton balls on the glue.

4. Sprinkle some of one of the extracts on the cotton balls.

5. Do the same with the other ice cream cone, using another extract. Mmmmm, the ice cream cones smell good enough to eat—but don't!

Going Further

Let's have an ice cream smelling party. Bring in ice cream with flavors that have very distinctive smell, such as strawberry, butter pecan, coffee, and chocolate. Have the children try to identify the flavors by using their sense of smell. Does anyone like the smell but not the taste of any particular ice cream?

Activity V-D3. Smell-and-Match Cards

Materials Needed

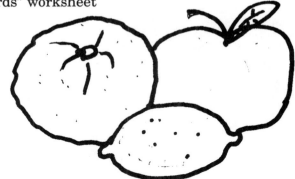

- copy of "Smell-and-Match Cards" worksheet
- four kinds of flavored gelatin:
    —lemon
    —orange
    —strawberry
    —grape
- oaktag
- markers or crayons
- glue
- scissors

Directions for Children

1. Color all the fruit on your worksheet.

2. Glue the worksheet onto the oaktag and cut the cards apart. Your teacher will help you with this.

3. Pick out one of the cards and look at the fruit shown. Now look at the boxes of gelatin. Which one has that fruit on it? Smell the gelatin.

4. Put a small amount of glue in the center of your fruit card and sprinkle some gelatin on the glue.

5. Do the same with the other fruit cards.

6. Now put all four cards in front of you. Close your eyes. Pick a card. Smell it. What fruit is it? Open your eyes. Were you right?

Going Further

Bring in some real fruit, such as apples, oranges, lemons, and grapefruit. Have the children use their sense of smell to identify each fruit. Then enjoy slices of these fruits at Snack Time.

Activity V-D4. A Bouquet of Perfumed Flowers

Materials Needed

- copy of "Bouquet of Perfumed Flowers" worksheet
- perfume or cologne
- markers or crayons
- scissors
- glue
- construction paper folded in half to make a card

Note to Teacher

Before doing this activity, be sure that no child has any allergies or conditions that can be affected by perfumes or colognes.

Directions for Children

1. Color each flower in the bouquet.
2. Cut around the bouquet and glue it on the front of the construction paper card. Your teacher will help you with this.
3. Lightly spray the card with perfume or cologne.
4. Your teacher will help you print a greeting inside the card for someone special.

Going Further

1. Bring in several different kinds of real flowers for the children to smell the varied scents.

2. Look up in the encyclopedia how perfume is made and share the explanation in very simple terms with the children.

Activity V-D5. Smell and Find

Materials Needed

- several supermarket flyers
- scissors
- one of each of the following in a sandwich bag:
    —piece of soap
    —scoop of ground coffee
    —tablespoon of cocoa mix
    —handful of popcorn

Note to Teacher

Explain that all of these items can be found in a supermarket in various kinds of packagings.

Directions for Children

1. Smell the contents of one of the bags. What do you think it is?
2. Look for that item in a supermarket flyer.
3. When you have found the picture, cut it out and put it in the bag with the real item.
4. Continue with the other smells.

Activity V-D6. Can You Tell the Cereal Smell?

Materials Needed

- variety pack of individual-sized cereal boxes
- four 6-inch squares of aluminum foil
- oaktag
- glue
- scissors

Note to Teacher

Select four different cereal boxes. Choose ones that smell differently from one another. Pour about half a box of cereal into the center of a piece of aluminum foil.

Roll the foil up and around the cereal to make a ball shape. Do the same for each cereal. Poke a few "smelling" holes into the aluminum.

Cut the front panel from each cereal box and glue them onto the oaktag.

Directions for Children

1. Smell one of the cereal balls.
2. Then look at the cereal box pictures. Can you guess which cereal it is?
3. Lay the cereal ball on its box picture.
4. Continue with the other cereal balls.

Going Further

Let the children sample these and other cereals at Snack Time. Do they like the tastes? Can they tell why?

Activity V-D7. Gelatin Smelling

Materials Needed

- one box each of three or four different flavors of gelatin
- small cups
- aluminum foil
- toothpick

Note to Teacher

Let the children help you make a variety of different flavors of gelatin. Then pour the gelatin into small cups and cover each cup with aluminum foil. Use a toothpick to make holes in the aluminum foil.

Directions for Children

1. Smell each cup and guess what flavor gelatin is in the cup.
2. Which smell do you like the best? Try to tell us why.

Going Further

Let the children sample these gelatin flavors at Snack Time. Do they like the tastes? Can they tell why?

V-E. TASTE

Purpose

Our sense of taste brings great pleasure to our lives. The children will use their tongues to taste nutritious foods of their own making.

Getting Started

Snack Time is a great time to begin your introduction to the sense of taste. Pass around a small mirror and let the children look at their tongues and the taste buds that cover the tongue.

Explain that all those many taste buds tell you the taste of your food, and that some parts of your tongue tell you the taste of sweet foods and other parts of your tongue taste the salty and sour foods.

Have the children taste a salty pretzel and a sweet piece of chocolate.

Activity V-E1. Cereal Sampling Party

Materials Needed

- cereal samples
- small plastic cups

Note to Teacher

Ask parents to send in a sandwich bag with their child of the child's favorite cereal to be sampled by the class.

Directions for Children

1. First, wash your hands. Then select five different kinds of cereal and fill five cups with a different cereal.
2. Now taste each of the cereals. Which one do you like best? Can you tell us why?

Going Further

Keep track of the children's favorite cereals by making a "cereal bar graph." Use the cereal pieces, oaktag, and glue to make the graph.

Activity V-E2. Make a Nutritious, Delicious Snack

Materials Needed

- two washed stalks of celery on a plastic plate
- peanut butter
- raisins
- plastic knife

Directions for Children

1. With your plastic knife, cut the celery stalks into bite-size pieces.
2. Fill the middle of each piece of celery with peanut butter.
3. Then put one raisin on top of each stuffed celery snack.
4. Pass the snacks around to your classmates. Don't forget to have one yourself!

Going Further

Stuff the celery pieces with whipped cream cheese. Can the children suggest other stuffings they might like to try?

Activity V-E3. My Tasting Plate

Materials Needed

- supermarket flyer
- paper plate
- scissors
- glue

Directions for Children

1. Look through the supermarket flyer at all the fruits, vegetables, meats, fish, cereals, and other foods that the supermarket sells.
2. Pick out pictures of things that you like to eat or would like to taste.
3. Cut out the pictures and glue them to your paper plate.

Going Further

1. Let the children volunteer to tell about what they had for dinner last night. What would their favorite dinner consist of?

2. Here are some tasty treats that the children can help make in the classroom:

Gelatin and Bananas

Prepare gelatin according to package directions. Alternate layers of gelatin and sliced (by the children) bananas in individual cups. Chill.

Cubed Gelatin

1 3-ounce package of gelatin
1 cup boiling water
3/4 cup cold water

Dissolve gelatin in boiling water. Add cold water and pour into a 9-inch square pan. Chill until firm. Cut with a sharp knife into cubes and remove with a spatula.

Grape Cream Delight

large bunch of grapes (at least 4 cups' worth)
1 cup sour cream
½ cup brown sugar

Have the children pick four cups of grapes off the bunch. Wash grapes. Mix the grapes together with the sour cream and brown sugar. Refrigerate for at least two hours or overnight. Serve in small cups.

Orange-Carrot Salad

1 package orange gelatin
1½ cups water
1 large carrot, shredded

Prepare gelatin using 1½ cups of water. Chill until gelatin is semi-firm; then stir in shredded carrots. Chill until firm.

Activity V-E4. A Good Cereal Chain

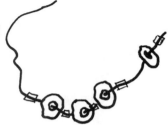

Materials Needed

- small bowl of Cheerios®
- ten 1-inch pieces of straw

- 18-inch piece of yarn with a large knot on one end
- plastic blunt needle (OR make the needle-end of the yarn stiff by wrapping cellophane tape tightly around the end, OR paint the end with clear nail polish)

Directions for Children

1. String on your yarn one of the small pieces of straw. Next, string on a Cheerio®.
2. Continue until you have used up all ten pieces of straw.
3. Tie the ends of the yarn together.
4. Reward yourself with some Cheerios® from the bowl.

Activity V-E5. Fruit Salad Snack

Materials Needed

- small banana
- apple wedges
- small bunch of grapes
- plastic plate
- plastic knife
- plastic bowl
- plastic fork
- napkins

Note to Teacher

Depending on the abilities of the children, they can either do all the cutting themselves (under your supervision, of course) or help you with the cutting.

Directions for Children

1. Peel the banana.
2. Put the banana on the plate and slice it into pieces with the plastic knife.
3. Put the banana slices in the bowl.
4. With your plastic knife, cut the apple wedges into small pieces.
5. Put the apples in the bowl with the bananas.
6. Pick about ten grapes off the bunch of grapes.
7. Put them in the bowl.

8. Gently mix your fruit with the knife.

9. Enjoy your fruit salad with your fork.

Activity V-E6. Finger Sandwich Tasting Party

Materials Needed

- lunch sandwiches
- platter
- paper plates
- napkins
- plastic knives
- raw vegetables (optional)

Note to Teacher

Ask parents to send with their child a lunch sandwich that will be shared with the class.

Cut the sandwiches into small triangles and rectangles. Lay these small finger sandwiches in an interesting pattern on a platter (and garnish with raw vegetables, if desired).

Directions for Children

Choose six finger sandwiches of different kinds and put them on your plate. Enjoy!

Activity V-E7. Tacos

Materials Needed

- plastic knives
- plastic spoons
- four bowls
- one pound ground beef browned and broken up into pieces (or use ground turkey, which is lower in fat and higher in protein)
- one cup mild taco sauce
- one cup shredded cheddar cheese
- one head lettuce, cut in wedges
- six tomatoes
- taco shells
- napkins

Note to Teacher

The children can help with many of these preparations: Wash the lettuce and shred it with the plastic knives. Put it in one of the bowls. Wash the tomatoes, cut them into wedges and then into small pieces, and put these into another bowl. Put the cheddar cheese into a third bowl and the ground beef into the fourth bowl.

Directions for Children

1. Here are the ingredients of a Mexican treat called a "taco."
2. Fill a taco shell with a little bit of each ingredient. Then put a little taco sauce on top.
3. Do you like the taste of the taco?

Going Further

Talk about other Mexican foods and try to make some available for tasting.

Activity V-E8. A Tasting Party for Rosh Hashanah

Note to Teacher

Celebrate the Jewish New Year with a tasting party. There are many delicious and interesting foods for the children to sample that are available in most supermarkets in the early fall:

Challah bread   Potato latkes
Gefilte fish   Blintzes
Halvah   Potato knishes or puffs
Chopped liver   Potato or apple pancakes
Matzo
Herring
Honey cake

TEACHER NOTES . . . .

TEACHER NOTES . . . .

TEACHER NOTES . . . .

TEACHER NOTES . . . .

TEACHER NOTES . . . .

TEACHER NOTES . . . .